CW01671707

ADOLF HITLER'S HOLIDAY SNAPS

German Aerial Reconnaissance Photography of Southern England 1939–1942

Avon
Cornwall
Devon
Dorset
Hampshire
Isle of Wight
Somerset

Nigel J. Clarke

ADOLF HITLER'S HOLIDAY SNAPS

German Aerial Reconnaissance Photography of Southern England 1939–1942

First published by Nigel J. Clarke Publications in 1995

Nigel J. Clarke Publications
Unit 2, Russell House,
Lym Close, Lyme Regis,
Dorset. DT7 3DE.
TEL: 01297 442513
FAX: 01297 442513

ISBN 0-907683-45-2

Design by Nigel J. Clarke Publications.
Typesetting by DP Photosetting, Aylesbury, Bucks.
Origination, printing and binding in Singapore,
under the supervision of MRM Graphics Ltd, Winslow, Bucks.

Thanks to Mr. Phillips of Exeter for the use of some of his photographs; Richard Holland of Uplyme, Lyme Regis for his help on German translations; and Mr. Chris Clarke for being cheaper than the bank.

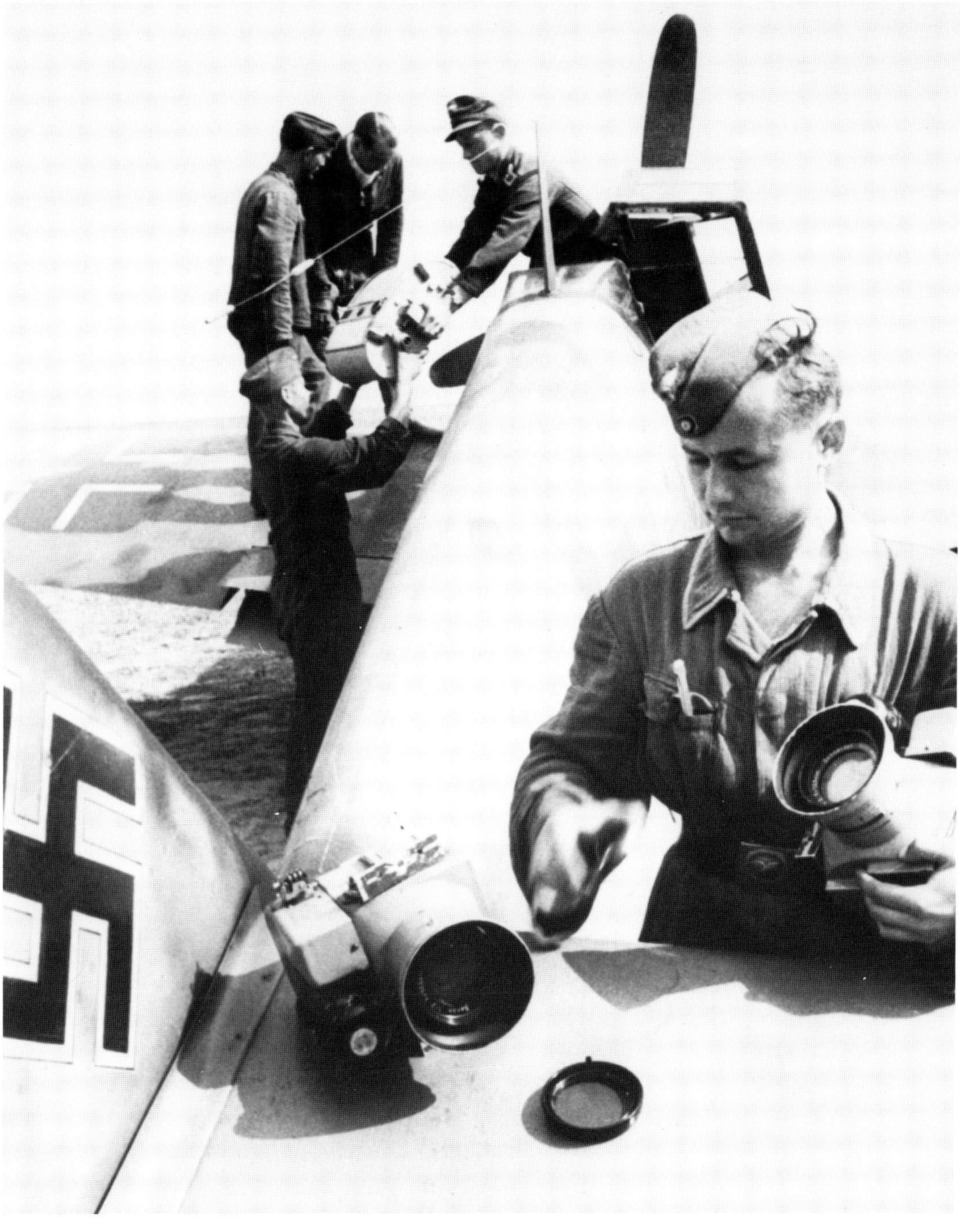

Messerschmitt 109 being loaded with reconnaissance camera and film at Dinard, St Malo. France

CONTENTS

INTRODUCTION

This book has taken three years to compile and represents only a small fraction of the aerial photographs taken by the Luftwaffe. My interest in the subject was first aroused after reading an article in a Sunday newspaper about the aerial photography undertaken by the German Airforce during World War II. I acquired a number of negatives of my own local area of Dorset from the collection. The aerial photographs were a window from the sky on to a country greatly changed over the last fifty years. I later expanded the collection to cover the entire United Kingdom and Ireland.

A local newspaper contacted me about the photographs, and printed a view of Weymouth, taken by the Luftwaffe in 1939, under the heading, 'Adolph Hitler's Dorset Holiday Snaps'. The interest in the photographs was immense, and I received numerous requests for copies of the photographs from individuals, museums and businesses. I also received many letters about the pictures, helping me fill in the background to the locations and subject of the photographs.

In the summer of 1994, I was contacted by a Mr Phillips, who had seen some photographs of Exeter taken by the Luftwaffe, which the local paper had published. During the Second World War, Mr Phillips's father had been a staff driver to General Horrocks, and had served throughout France and Germany. Towards the end of the war, while waiting for the General at a newly liberated Luftwaffe airfield in northern France, Mr. Phillips decided to explore some of the subterranean command bunkers, abandoned by the German airforce. The airfield had been hurriedly evacuated and many of the rooms were littered with documents. In one of the bunkers was an operations briefing room, and scattered about were hundreds of photographs of the west of England. Staff driver Phillips filled his tunic up with the most interesting and at the end of the war brought the photographs back to his home in Devon. The photographs were soon forgotten and left to gather dust, in an old box, on the top shelf, behind the counter at a small agricultural merchants shop, in Exeter.

Mr Phillips died in 1993 and his son discovered the dusty box containing the collection of photographs, and telephoned me after reading the article in his local newspaper about the collection of aerial photographs that I had. I was able to examine these unique prints, and have been allowed to include them in this book, for which I am grateful.

The aerial photographs in this book were taken over fifty years ago. My initial interest had little to do with the military aspects of the photographs. I was more interested in how the landscape had changed; cliffs had crumbled, villages had grown, the urbanisation of vast areas of our cities, the loss of small fields and the grubbing out of old hedgerows. I was also greatly suprised at the level of interest in the photographs and was approached by a variety of people, from town planners to individuals who just wanted to see the area where their house was built, to others looking for soil contamination from old abandoned industries. One of the most unusual inquiries for a copy of one of the prints came from the Wildfowler's Association at Poole. Some of their senior members lamented the disappearance and changes in the marshes and wetlands of Poole Harbour. They had no proof of these changes till one of their members contacted me about some of what I had thought were the more boring aerial photographs of the bog and marsh on Poole Harbour's western side. The recollections of the senior wildfowler's were correct; by the comparing of these old photographs with recent aerial survey photography, the amount of bog and marsh could be seen to have deminished. The reasons and causes for this environmental change are for someone else, more learned than me, to fathom.

With typical Teutonic thoroughness, the German Luftwaffe had undertaken the first ever aerial survey of the United Kingdom. Most of the portfolio in this book are German target photographs and contain the information of most interest to the German intelligence services. The photographs are annotated with information as to the target subject, location, and the time that the pictures were taken. There are other aerial survey pictures of the United Kingdom but all date after the Second World War and by then much of Britain had changed forever.

A BRIEF HISTORY OF AERIAL PHOTOGRAPHY

The first aerial photographs were taken from a balloon at the turn of the century. Its usefulness soon became apparent to military planners, and during the First World War it was employed by all sides, though confined mainly to the battle fronts.

The pioneers in Britain were Major W.G. Allen and O.G.S. Crawford in the 1930's, who showed how aerial photography could be used as a tool in landscape research.

It was not until the Second World War that the Luftwaffe started the systematic photographic recording of Great Britain, the first ever co-ordinated recording of the country from the air. The Royal Air Force made aerial photographic surveys after the war.

Today, our landscape is photographed from space as well as from planes. Agriculture, archaeology, planning and road building are among the many uses of aerial photography.

THE LUFTWAFFE RECONNAISSANCE

Most of the collection of photographs in this book were taken between 1939 and 1943. The German command had realised early in the in the war the importance of up to date aerial intelligence, and the Blitzkrieg tactic called for pinpoint bombing of targets to disrupt the supply lines and industrial strata of the defending country. The Luftwaffe were well prepared for the attack on the United Kingdom. Their aircraft had been flying over the country, at high altitude, prior to the declaration of war. The clarity of the images is exceptional. The German airforce had developed special aerial cameras and commissioned the Carl Zeiss company to build them. The planes flew to a height of up to 37,000 ft, observing and photographing targets. The film was then taken back to their bases, developed and collated. The Germans used the photographs in conjunction with the British Ordnance Survey map (one inch to one mile). Extracts of the map and copies of the target photographs were then supplied to the bomber crews.

After the fall of France and the allied retreat from Dunkirk, the German high command proposed the invasion of the United Kingdom. Intelligence was required of possible landing sites and the coastal defences of southern England. The German high command planned that the 6th Army would depart from Cherbourg and attempt landings at Weymouth and in the Lyme Bay area, and then go on to occupy Devon and Cornwall.

Generalfeldmarschall Hermann Goering, the commander-in-chief of the Luftwaffe, promised Adolf Hitler complete German domination of the air. The German High Command planned for the invasion of Britain after the fall of France. The initial stages of the operation were to be the elimination of the Royal Air Force as an effective fighting group, and the disruption of all marine and port activities. This first phase of the proposed German invasion was fought in the skies above England.

At the outbreak of the Battle of Britain, the Luftwaffe allocated 2,600 aircraft for the operations against the UK. The reconnaissance section consisted of 140 aircraft, with a further 30 available from the Norwegian sector. The initial reconnaissance missions were undertaken by Dornier bombers* to establish the potential strength of the defending British forces. These initial flights were solo missions, and the Luftwaffe reconnaissance planes also dropped flares and small incendiaries to try and goad the Royal Air Force into action.

By 1941, after suffering tremendous losses and with the start of the war on the Russian front, all thoughts of a British invasion by the Germans had disintegrated. The Luftwaffe had suffered its first major defeat of the war, and the resources of men and aircraft were no longer available for the western sector of German operations. Many of the front line units were transferred to the invasion of Russia and eastern Europe.

The aerial reconnaissance flights continued throughout the war. The Germans routinely monitored the country for troop movements and for the selection of bombing targets. Towards the end of the war, the Germans searched for the embarkation points, prior to the D-day landings, but the aircraft available for reconnaissance missions were few and the skies of Britain were well protected by fighters.

The South West received a great deal of bomb damage. The naval centres of Plymouth , Portsmouth and Portland were regular targets. The economic centres of Bristol. Southampton, Poole and Exeter were blitzed, and potential military targets were regularly photographed.

At the end of the war vast quantities of intelligence material were captured by the allies. The American Forces captured the main central records of the Luftwaffe, and set up a joint allied operation to collate and sort the information. The material was transferred to R.A.F Medmemham and the subsequent project was named Operation Dick Tracy. The information obtained from this project was shared by the joint allied commanders.

*The Dornier bomber had originally been built as an experimental high speed mail plane for trials with the German civil airline Lufthansa. The aeroplane was an all-metal construction with a maximum ceiling height of 26,400 ft, and a maximum speed of 265 mph. The plane was rejected by Lufthansa, despite its then exceptional performance, because of the difficulty passengers had entering its two small cabins. The aircraft were returned to Dornier and stored in a hangar, where they were seen by a Luftwaffe evaluation pilot. After a trial flight, Flugkapitan Robert Untucht was so impressed with the handling and design that he recommended the plane's design as the basis of a new German bomber and reconnaissance aircraft. Also used on the reconnaissance missions over Britain was a twin engine aircraft, the Junkers 88 and the single engine fighter the Messerschmitt 109.

R.A.F. MEDMENHAM

The British were slow in realising the importance of aerial reconnaissance and most of the pre-war war spying was undertaken by the Secret Service, using freelance agents. The most notable was an Australian businessman Sidney Cotton. Mr Cotton was also a pilot who flew his own plane on regular trips over Italy, Germany and the occupied territories during the 1930's. His plane had been specially adapted by the British Secret Service with hidden cameras to take over-head reconnaissance photographs.

The Royal Air Force had few aircraft, or the capability for aerial reconnaissance until 1939, and it was only the outbreak of war and the threat of a possible invasion from the coast of Northern France that caused the R.A.F. to set up a specialist unit, which was eventually stationed at R.A.F. Medmenham. The unit co-ordinated the work and interpretation of reconnaissance missions all over the European operations area. Specially adapted planes such as Spitfires and Mosquitoes were used for these operations. New cameras were designed; one had enough film available in its magazine for 500 exposures and was capable of producing a scaled image of 1:10,000 taken at 30,000 ft.

The amount of work handled by Medmenham was phenomenal. In 1942 the station processed over 1.5 million photographs, and on one day developed 18,979 prints. Most of the Luftwaffe aerial records were sent to Medmenham at the end of the War for processing and assessment by the joint Anglo-American intelligence unit, under the code name of Operation Dick Tracy.

THE COUNTIES COVERED IN THIS BOOK:-

AVON

The main section of photographs are of Bristol and the surrounding area. The Germans were interested in the docks and city industries. The port at Avonmouth is also shown with its adjacent metal works and grain silos. At Portishead Down the army had established an anti-aircraft training area. The water reservoir at Long Ashton is the main water source for the city of Bristol and was also a target.

CORNWALL

The only photo in this collection is of Penzance and Newlyn. The harbour can clearly be seen, and both ports were designated German targets.

DEVON

The coastline and towns of Devon were regularly over-flown by the reconnaissance aircraft of the Luftwaffe. Plymouth was a major Naval base. Devonport had dockyards, repair facilities, ammunition stores and barracks. Much of Plymouth has changed in the last fifty years; familiar landmarks such as the railway stations at Millbay and Devonport have disappeared, and the Naval dockyards now have a frigate re-fitting complex.

The Southwest was an easy target for the German raiders, and during the early part of the war there was little defence from the depleted ranks of the Royal Airforce. The Air Council, in an assessment of the possibility of bombing , concluded that the risk of the South West being bombed by the Luftwaffe was slight . The assessment was made in 1938 when the Council thought that any German bombers would be flying from German bases, never thinking that France would collapse and that bombers would fly from bases along Europe's western shores.

Most of the towns suffered bomb damage, with Plymouth and Exeter being regular targets. The losses of life and buildings were at their greatest in Plymouth, which suffered some of the worst damage of any British city during the war.

Devon has change greatly in the past fifty years. In 1931, the total population of Devon was 732,968 and declining. Communications were poor, and most major local industries apart from tourism were in recession. The farms were small with only twelve holdings in the whole of Devon having more than 500 acres. The average farm had a herd of only ten cows. The war brought a boom to Devon. It was the most militarised county in England with a large influx of servicemen and an estimated 82,000 evacuees resident in the county.

Since the war, Plymouth, Exeter and Torbay's conurbations have all grown. Many sleepy villages have had new housing estates added to them, farms have grown larger, and roads have improved and motor ways been built.

DORSET

The Dorset coastline was at one time selected as a possible invasion point for the German forces, though towards the end of the war it became a centre and gathering zone for the allied forces that liberated Europe. Bournemouth, Poole, Portland and Weymouth became embarkation centres for the allied troops as they crossed over to the beaches for the D-Day landings.

The changes and expansion of the towns and villages in the east of the county have been dramatic. The combined populations of Poole and Bournemouth in 1931 stood at 177,000. Today the population is nearer 300,000 . In the aerial photo of Poole and Bournemouth you can still see an area of farmland separating these two towns. This area is now developed and a visitor would have great difficulty deciding where Poole finishes and Bournemouth starts.

Further along the coast of Dorset you come to some of the most unstable cliffs to be found in the United Kingdom. The aerial photograph of Lyme Regis shows the golf course and cliffs of Black Ven. On the cliffs can be seen a road that has now been pushed over the edge and lost to the sea. In the aerial photograph of Dorchester , Maiden Castle can be identified in the topmost corner, a useful marker for any pilot. The harbour of Portland was one of the first areas in Britain to suffer from the German bombers , though given the amount of quarrying it is difficult to distinguish between bomb damage and the self-inflicted wounds on the landscape from stone extraction. Swanage is just a small sleepy coastal village. The local home guard, in an effort to deny the German forces the landing facilities of the short stubby pier, had demolished the connecting section to the land.

HAMPSHIRE AND THE ISLE OF WIGHT

Geographically Hampshire and the Isle of Wight were primary targets for the Luftwaffe. The area was regularly bombed and photographed. In order for the Germans to invade southern England, and for the invasion to be successful, the Royal Navy needed to be bombed out of the bases along the south coast. Portsmouth was the largest Naval base in Britain and nearby were the Fleet Air Arm stations at Lee-on-Solent and Gosport. On the Isle of Wight there were aircraft factories at Cowes, such as Vickers-Supermarine, which was one of the major factories producing Spitfires. At the end of the war, over 10,000 buildings had bomb damage on the Isle of Wight, while the centres of Portsmouth and Southampton had been reduced to rubble and changed forever.

Since the end of the Second World War, the commercial centres of Portsmouth and Southampton have been rebuilt, the population has grown, and with it have come vast new areas of housing.

SOMERSET

The war in Somerset came from the skies. The Luftwaffe made regular reconnaissance flights over the county, and the first large-scale bombing occurred on the 10th of July 1940, yet Somerset remained relatively unscathed till the 15th of July when a small force of German bombers attacked RNAS Yeovilton and the Westland Aircraft Company at Yeovil.

Mr Gerald Little recalls the early reconnaissance flights by the Luftwaffe... 'Enemy reconnaissance aircraft were often seen flying overhead – they were photographing the Westland Aircraft factory. At the start of the war, new hangars were under construction and they set a warning red light on the main building works. When the light was turned on and a hooter went off, you knew a reconnaissance aircraft was about. Everyone on the site had to rush off and collect corrugated sheets from a big pile, kept near-by, which we lay on the new concrete floors of the hangers, so that the symmetry of the newly laid white concrete would be broken.'

Other targets such as Weston-Super-Mare and Taunton were bombed as the Luftwaffe returning from missions over Bristol randomly dropped any spare bombs.

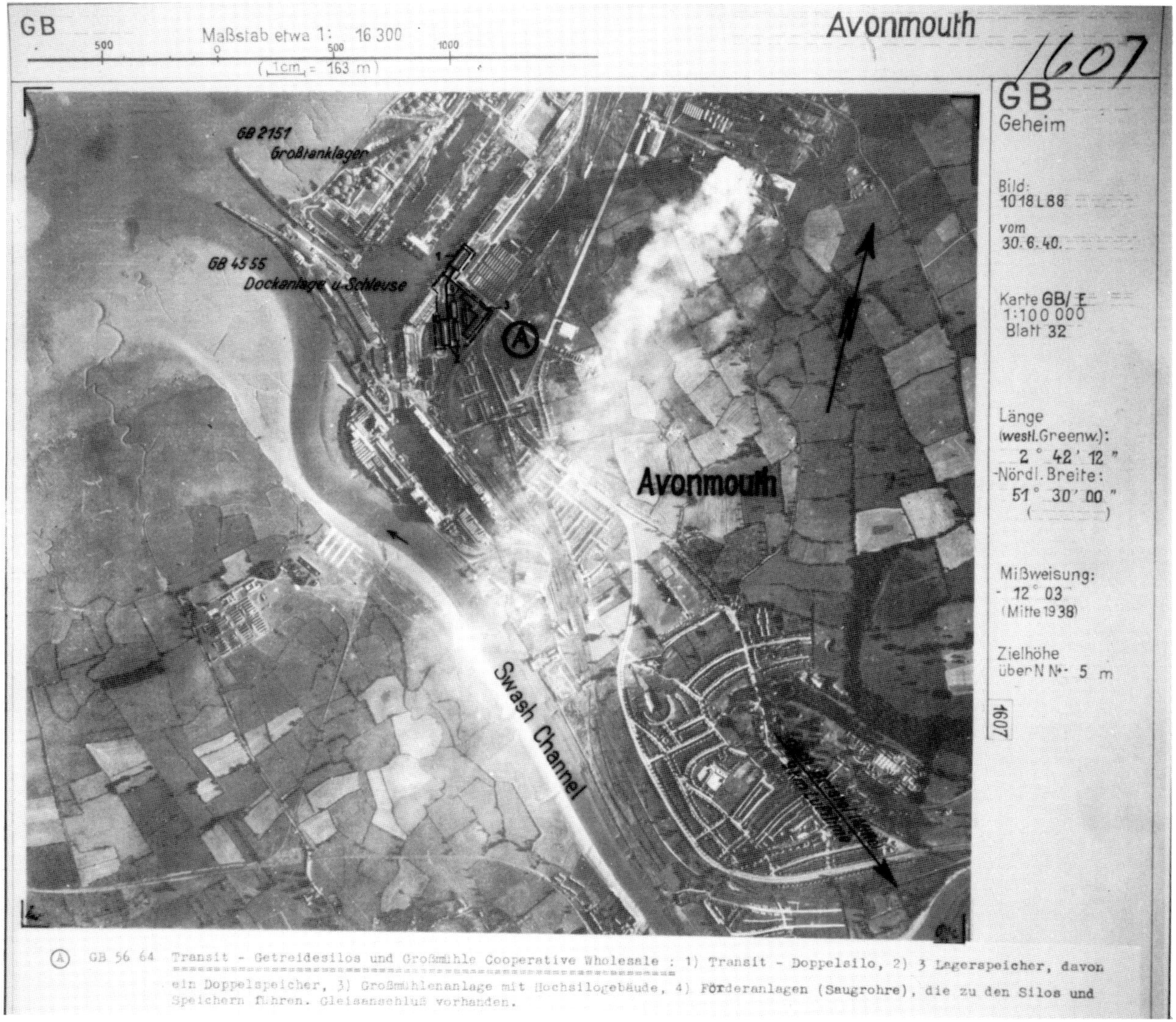

Avon Avonmouth
30th June 1940
Grain Silos and Docks
TN 1607
Comment

The ports of Bristol, Portishead and Avonmouth became vitally important, and became a primary target for the German bombers. Despite numerous attacks by the Luftwaffe the ports remained in operation throughout the war.

AVONMOUTH & BRISTOL

GB 179 bc N. f. D.	**Bristol (Whitchurch)** Peilanlage	Karte 1:100 000 Engl. Bl. 32 b

Bild Nr. 288 Z 10 **Geogr. Lage** 2° 35′ W, 51° 25′ N, **Höhe ü. d. M.** 65 m **Stand** VIII. 40.

500 0 500 1000 m

Maßstab etwa 1: 16 000 (1 cm = 160 m)

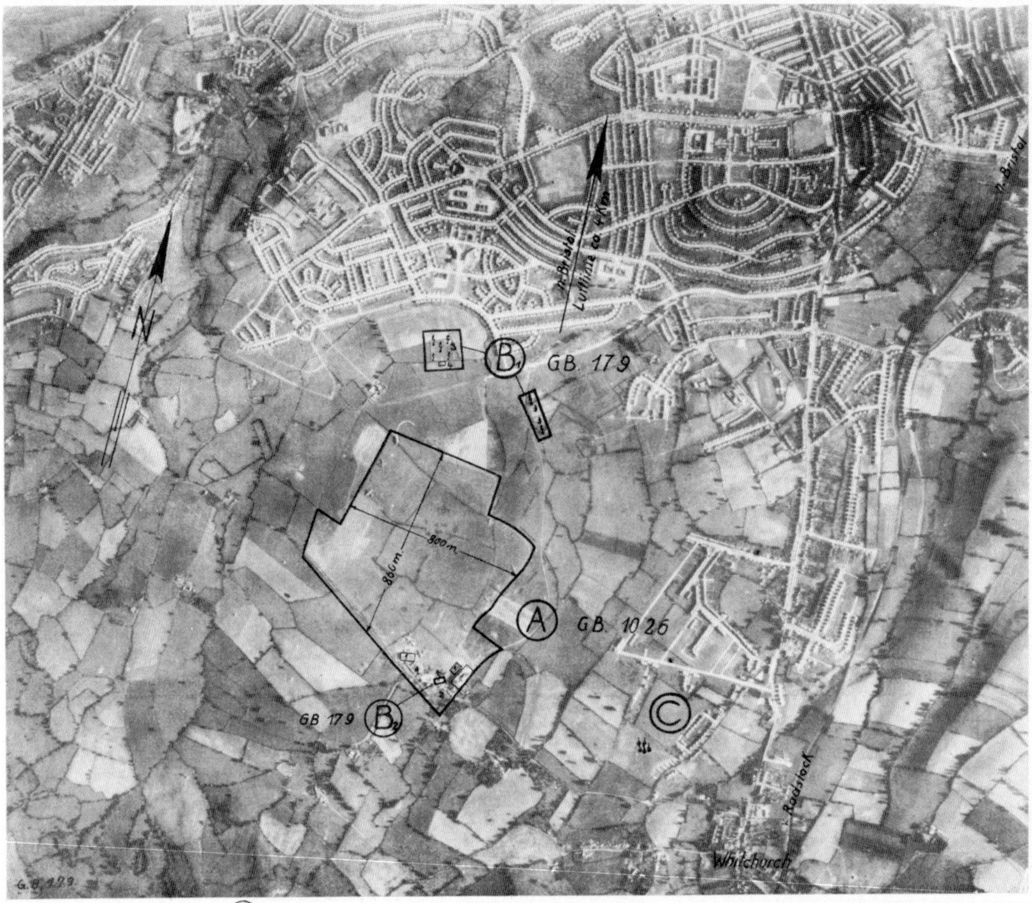

(A) GB 10 26 Flugplatz 800 x 860 m
1) 3 Flugzeughallen
2) Verwaltungs- und Nebengebäude

(B1) (B2) GB 17 9 Peilanlage
3) 7 Sendemaste
4) Betriebsgebäude

(C) ______ Flakstellung (leichte Flak)

Bristol
August 1940
Airfield
GB 179
Comment
Bristol had a concentration of aircraft manufacturers such as Parnall, at Yate and The Bristol Aeroplane Company. Both factories were regular targets, though output of planes increased during the war.

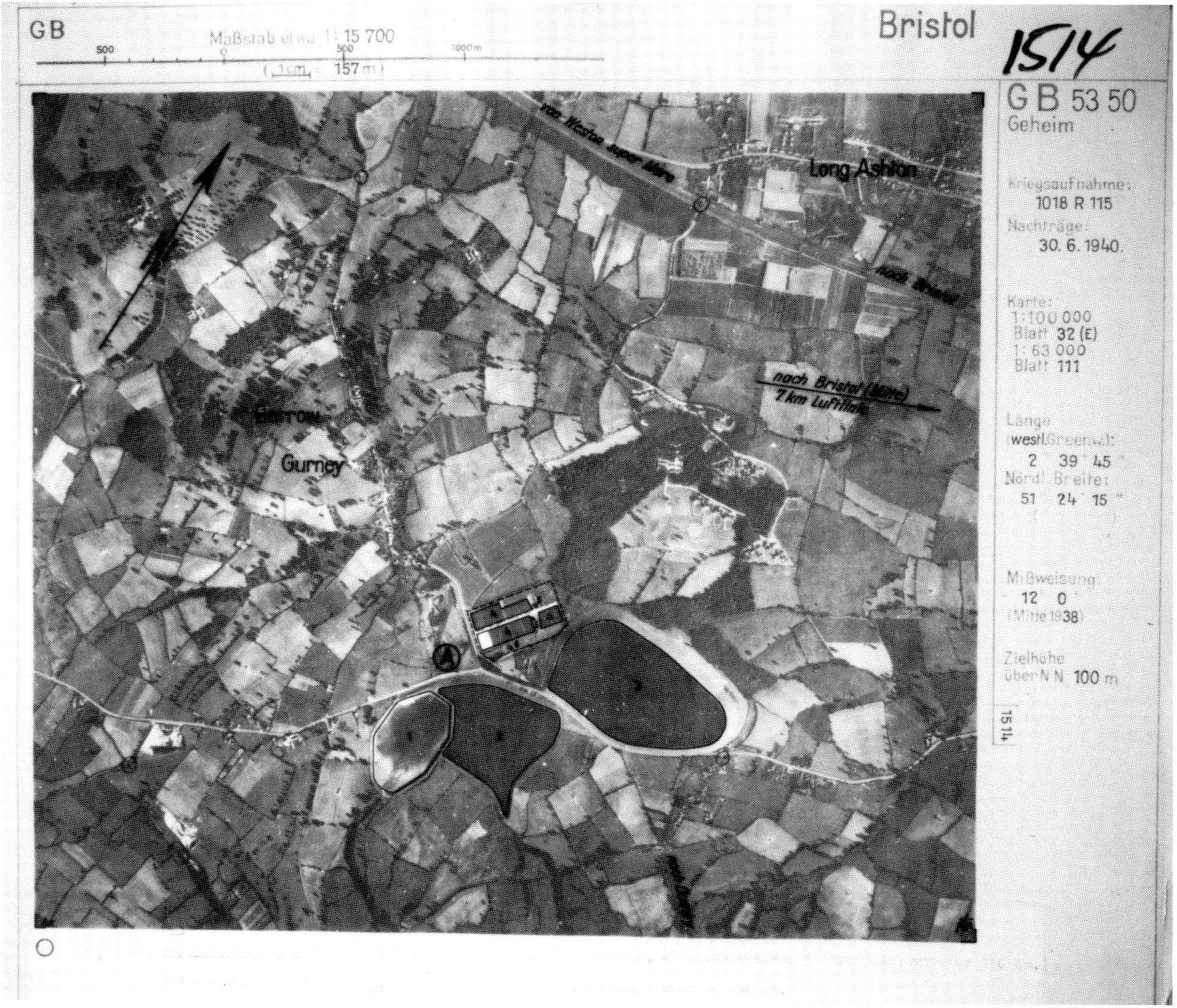

Bristol
30th June 1940
Water Reservoir at Long Ashton and village of Barrow Gurney.
TN 1514
Comment
During the defence of Bristol from air attack the army fired 59,741 shells and rockets at the Luftwaffe. A total of 96 German aircraft were destroyed and 240 German airmen lost their lives over Bristol. The city was the fourth most bombed city in Britain between August 1940 and June 1941. Only London, Liverpool and Birmingham had more tons of explosives dropped on them. The bombs killed 1,243 civilians and injured nearly three thousand.

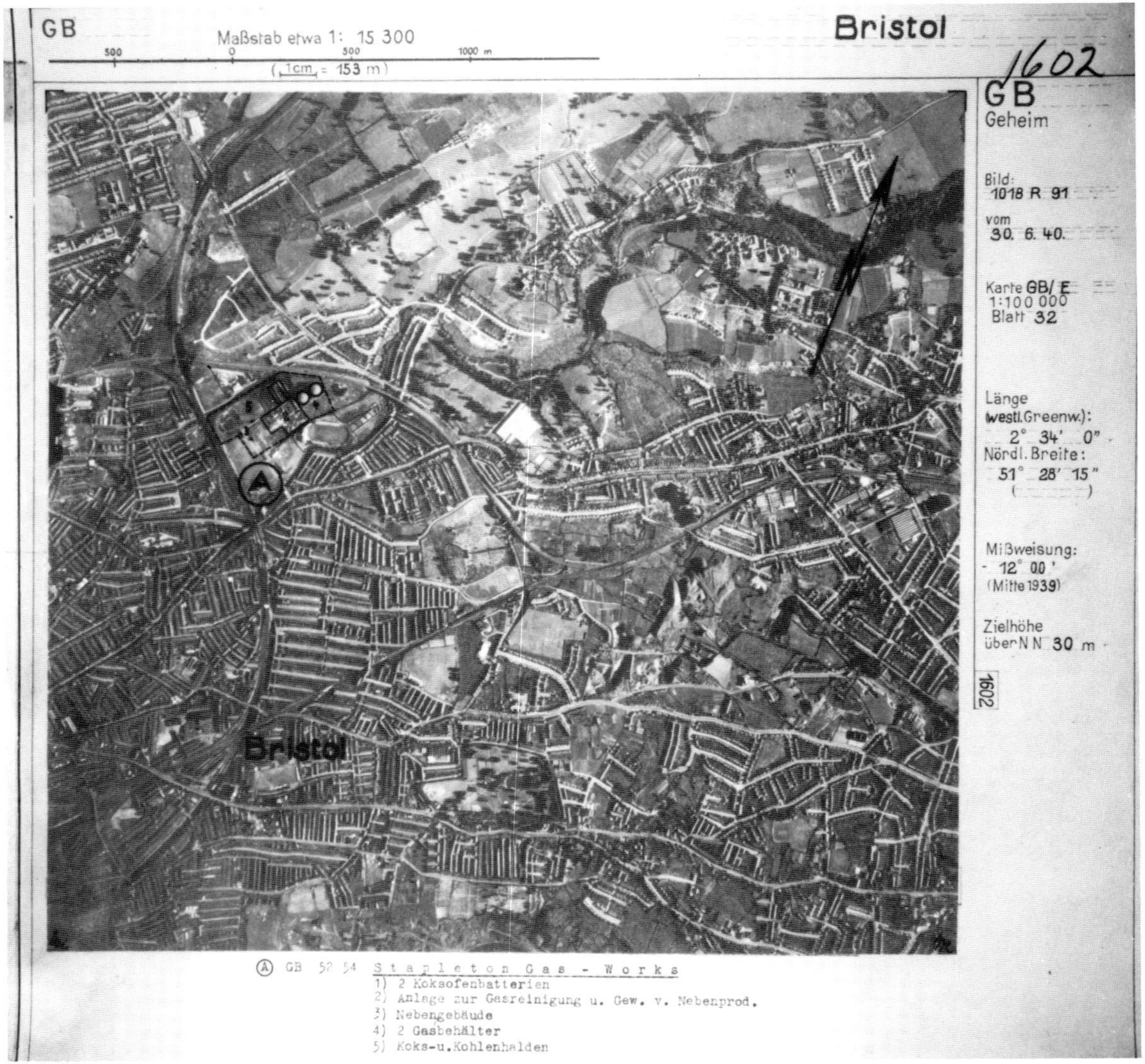

Bristol
30th June 1940
Stapleton Gas Works
TN 1602
Comment

The first major air attack on Bristol occurred on the 24th November 1940. The bombs fell in a line from Chard, in Somerset, to Bristol. The city suffered heavy damage, with the commercial and shopping areas of Wine Street and Castle Street being completely destroyed during the attack. The ancient churches of St Nicholas, St Peter's and St Mary-le-Port were all gutted and destroyed. The air raid killed over 200 people and 698 were injured. Further large scale bombing attacks occurred on the 2nd and 6th of December. These two raids killed a further 356 people and injured nearly a thousand more civilians.

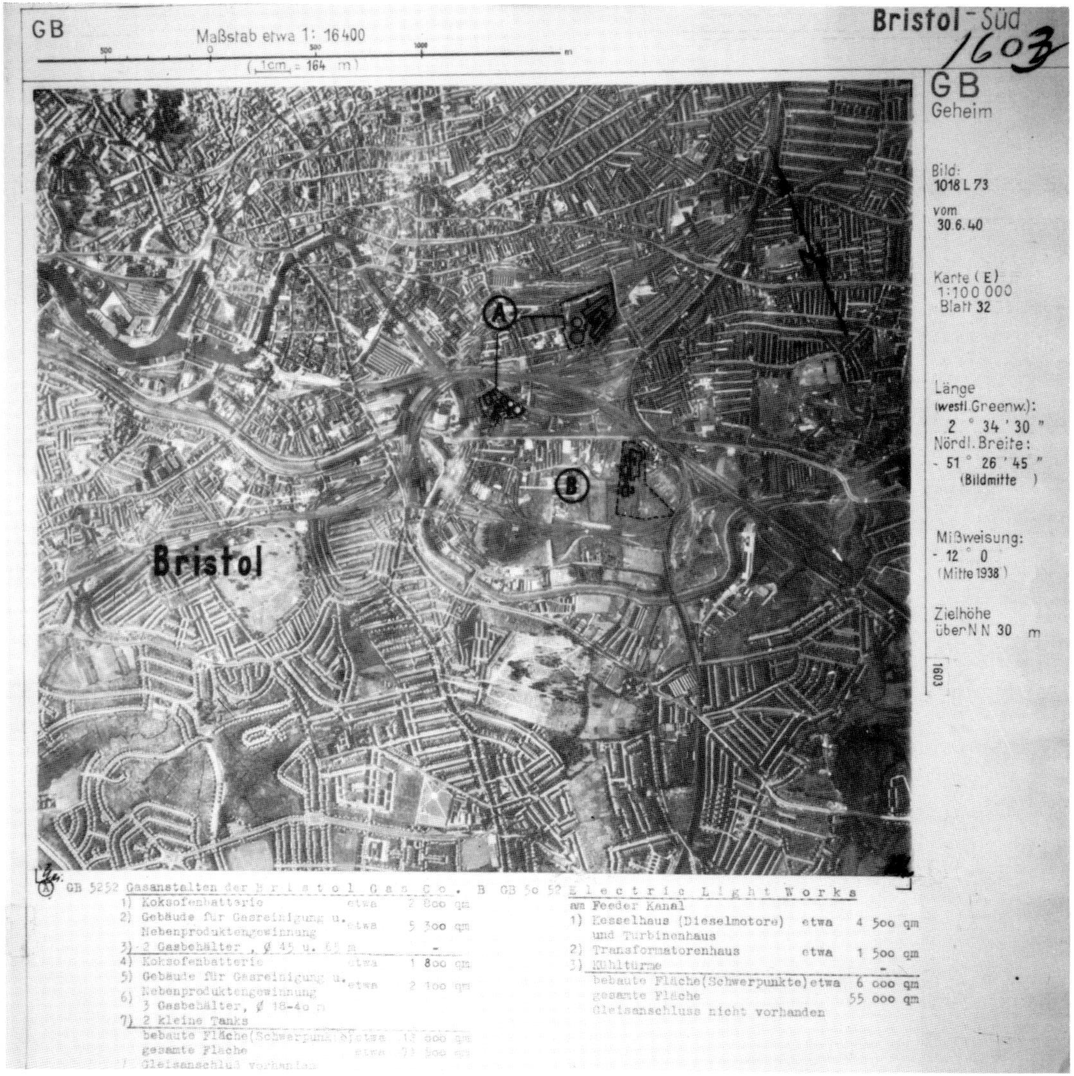

Bristol
30th June 1940
Bristol Gas Works and the Electricity Station.
TN 1603
Comment
On the 3rd January, 1941, Bristol sustained twelve hours of continues air attack, which killed 149 people and injured 351. The last major attack on Bristol was on April 11th, 1941, when two raids killed 180 civilians. Bristol had a large number of barrage balloons to protect vital industries and the docks. The value of such defensive manners to protect industries was doubtful as many thought you might as well plant a large flag on the site saying bomb me. The balloons would have deterred machine gunning and dive bombers but had little effect on the blitz of the Luftwaffe.

Bristol
30th June 1940
The Floating Harbour, Albion and Wapping Docks
TN 1604

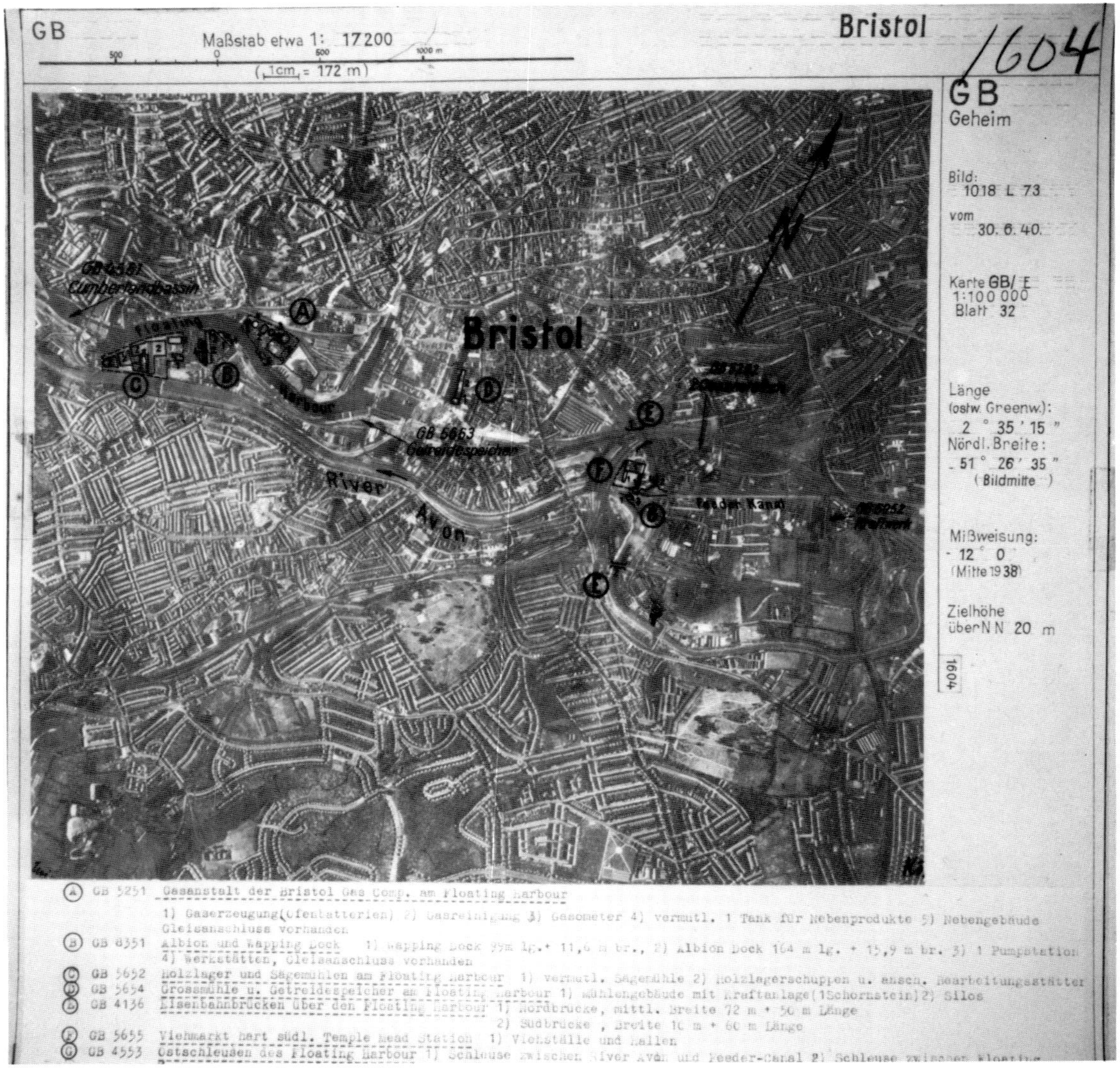

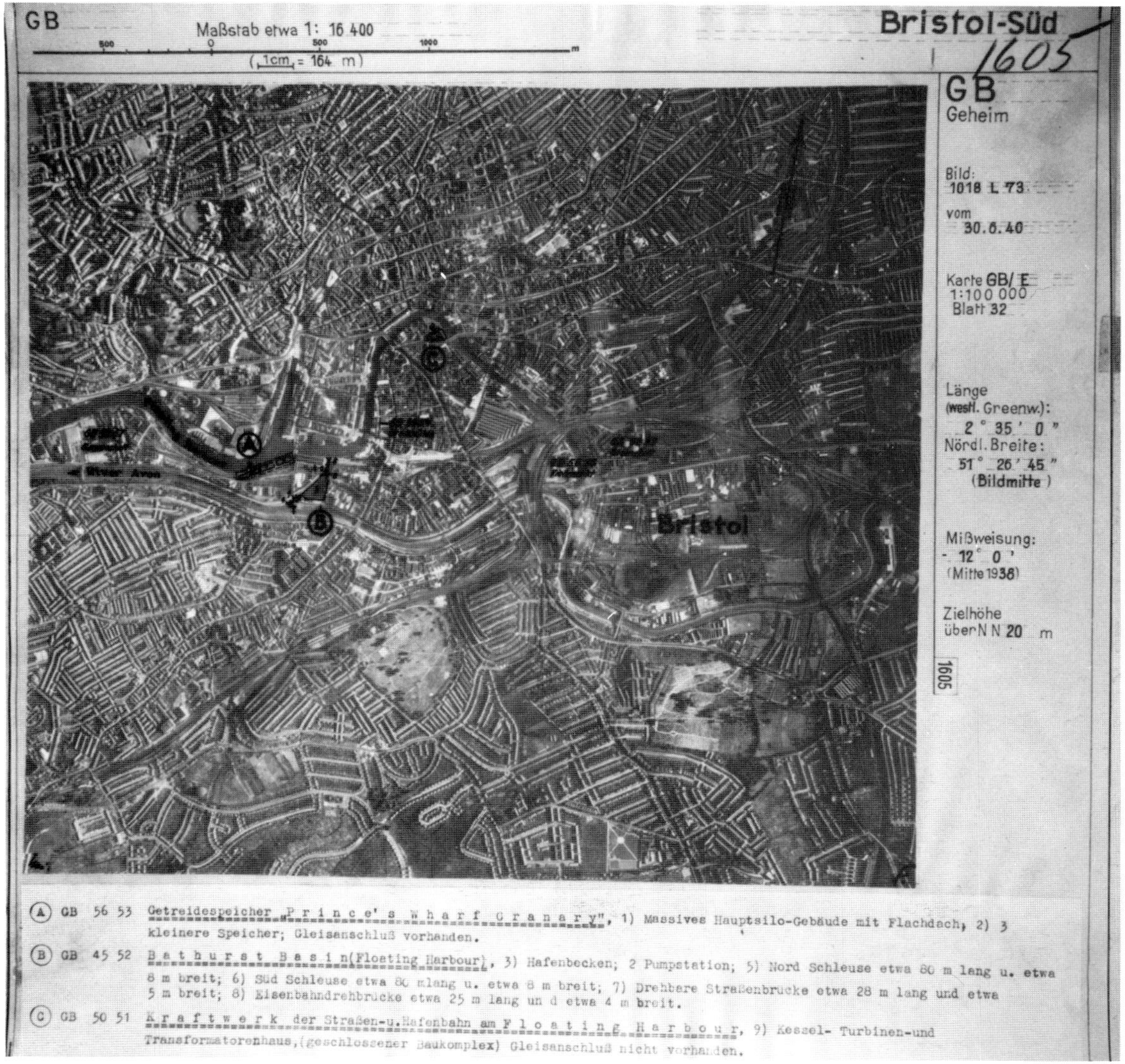

Bristol
30th June 1940
Floating Harbour, Bathurst Wharf and Princes Wharf Granary
TN 1605

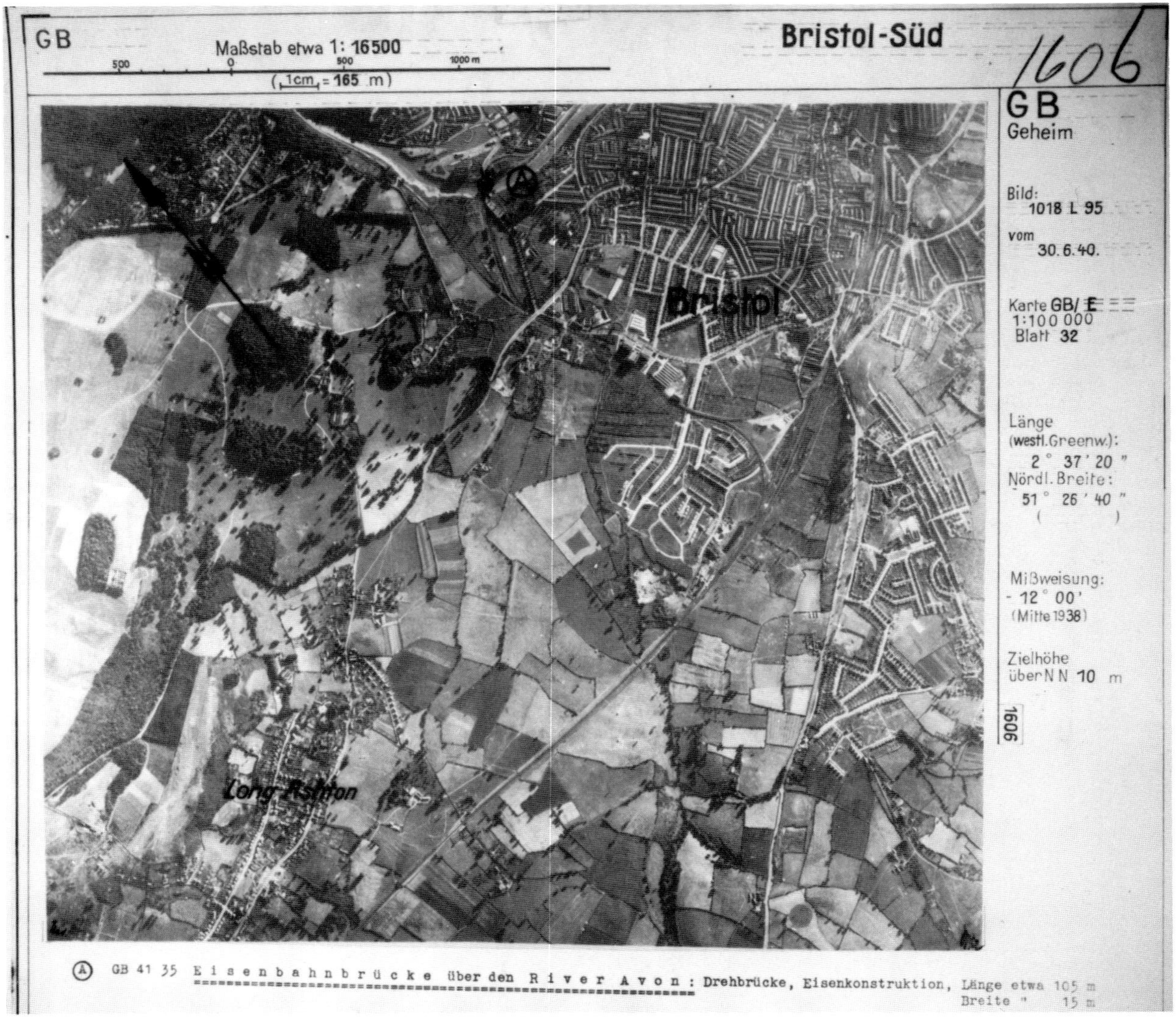

Bristol

30th June 1940

Feeder canal from the River Avon to the Floating Harbour.

TN 1606

Comment

At the end of the war the city authorities estimated that 89,080 properties had been damaged by the bombing and 3,092 buildings had been totally destroyed.

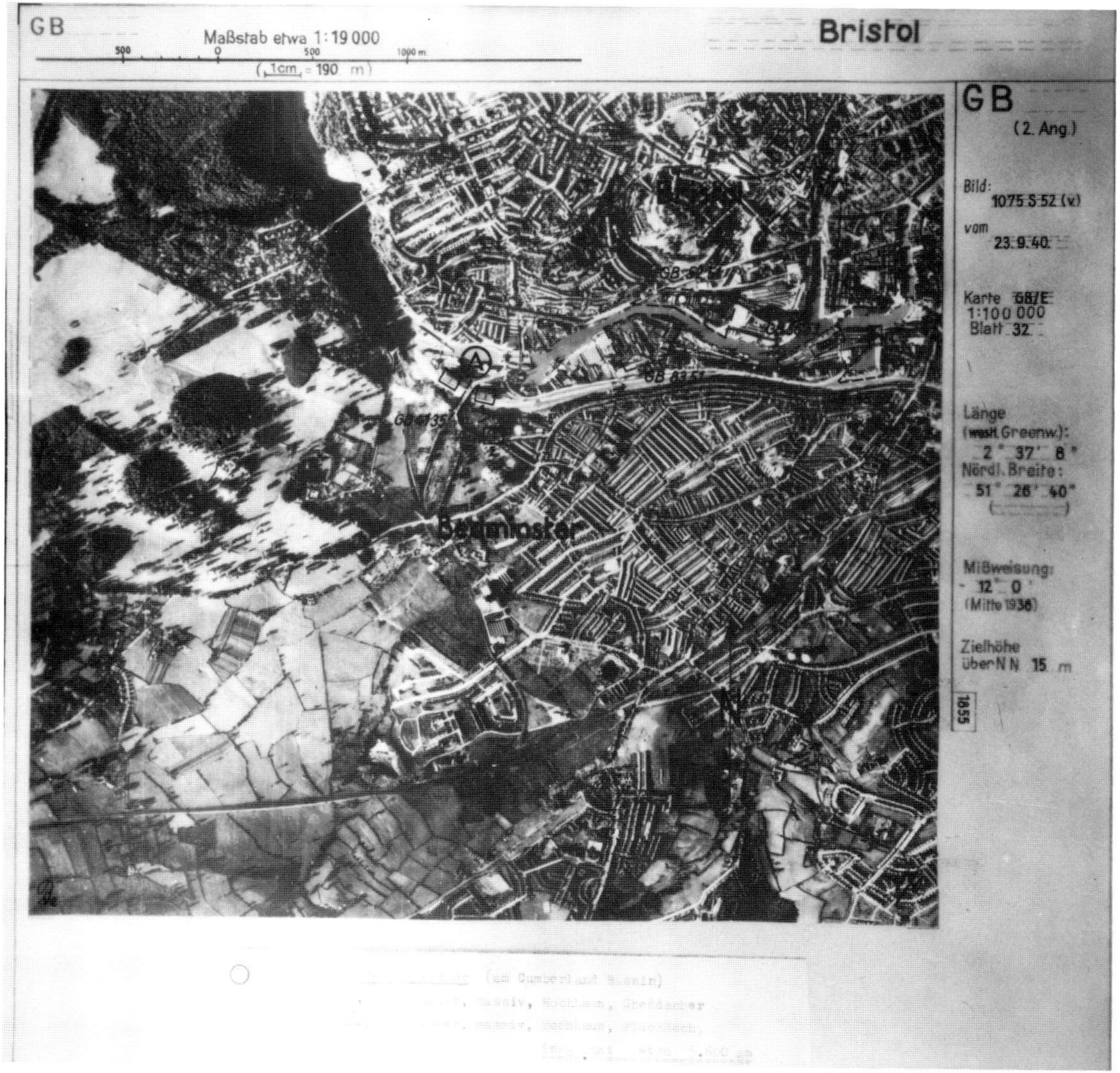

Bristol
23rd September 1940
Bedminster, Cumberland Basin and Clifton
TN 1855

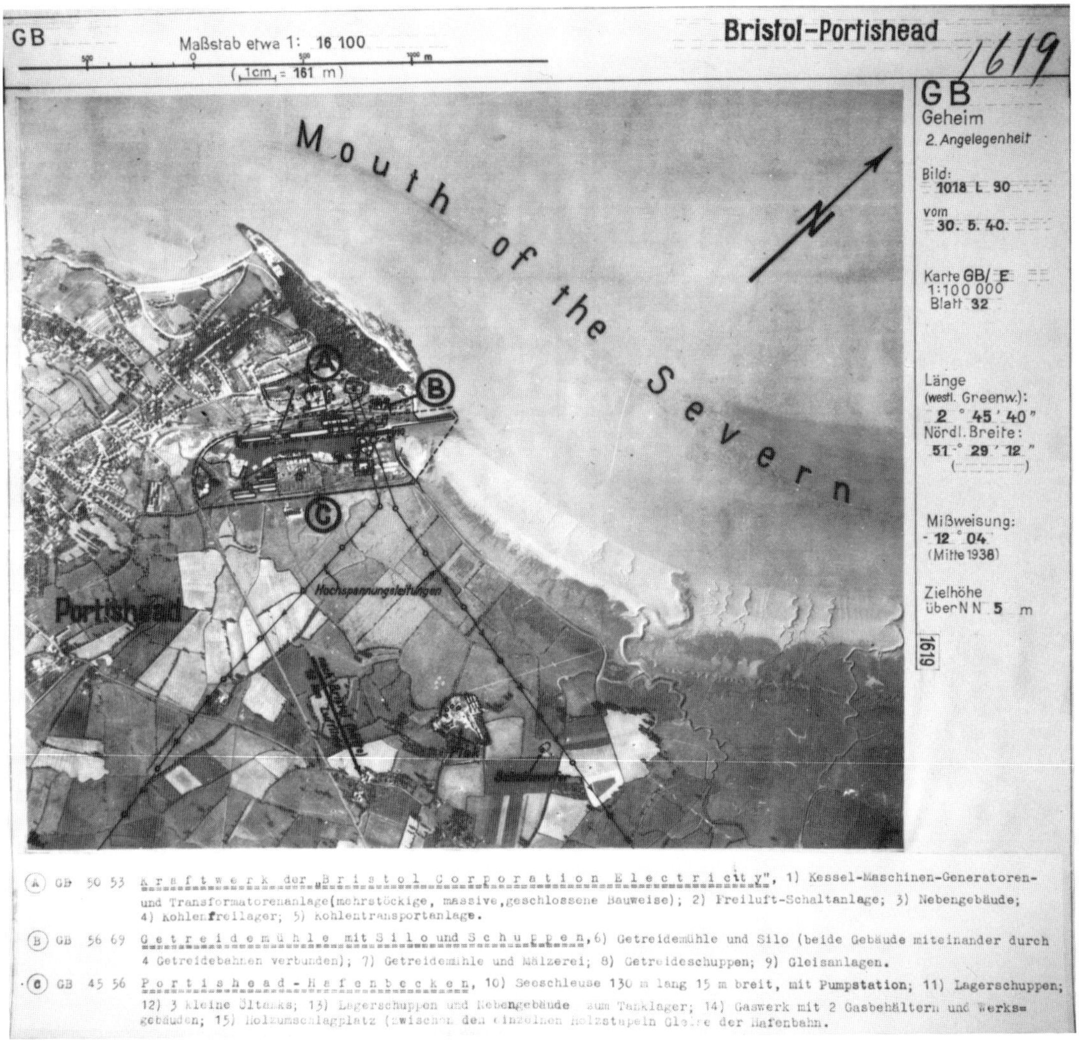

Portishead
30th May 1940
Power Station, Grain Silos and Docks
TN 1619
Comment
The only troops to sail from Somerset, for the D-day landings, were two divisions that embarked from Portishead. At Portishead were the 6-inch guns of the coastal defence battery.

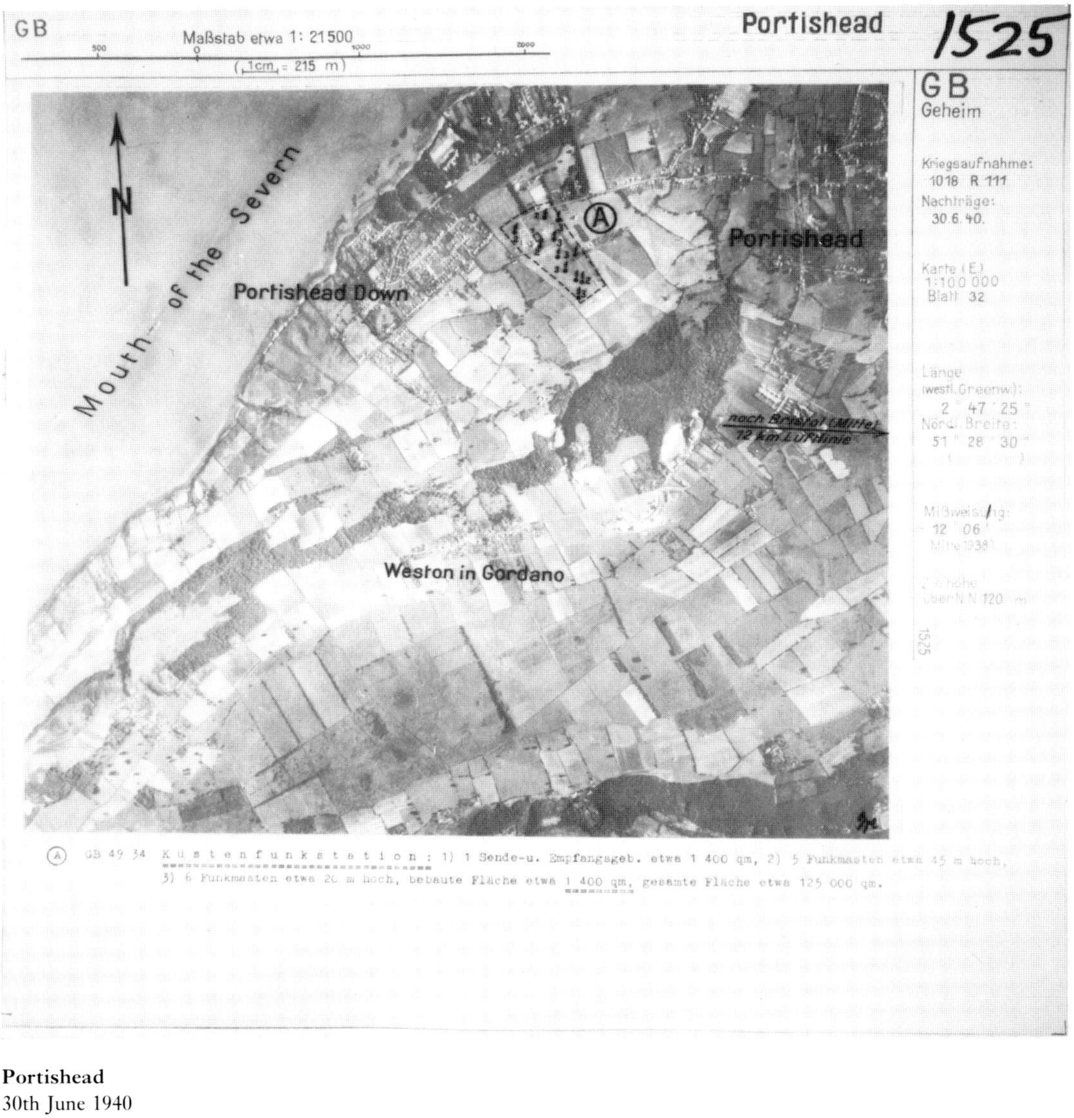

Portishead
30th June 1940
Wireless Station and Portishead Down
TN 1525

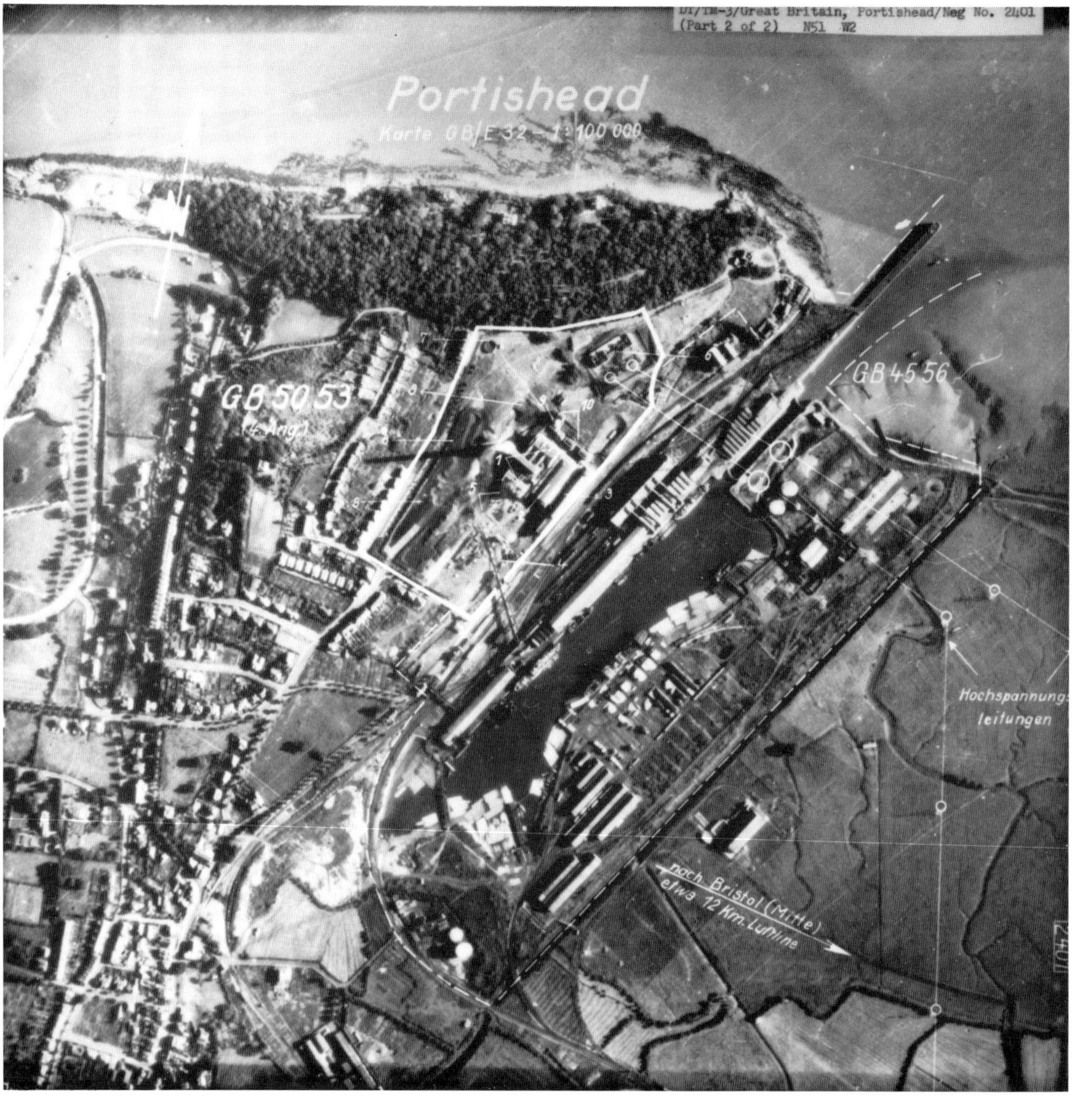

Portishead
30th June 1940
Power Station and Docks
TN 2401

GB 45 187 b c
N. f. D.

Penzance
Hafenanlage

Karte 1 : 100 000
Engl. Bl. 35 c

Bild Nr. F 1014b/40/257 Geogr. Lage: 5° 32' W, 50° 07' N, Höhe ü. d. M. — m Stand: III. 41.
v. 8.11.40

Maßstab etwa 1 : 10 000 (1 cm = 100 m) Lfl. Kdo. 3

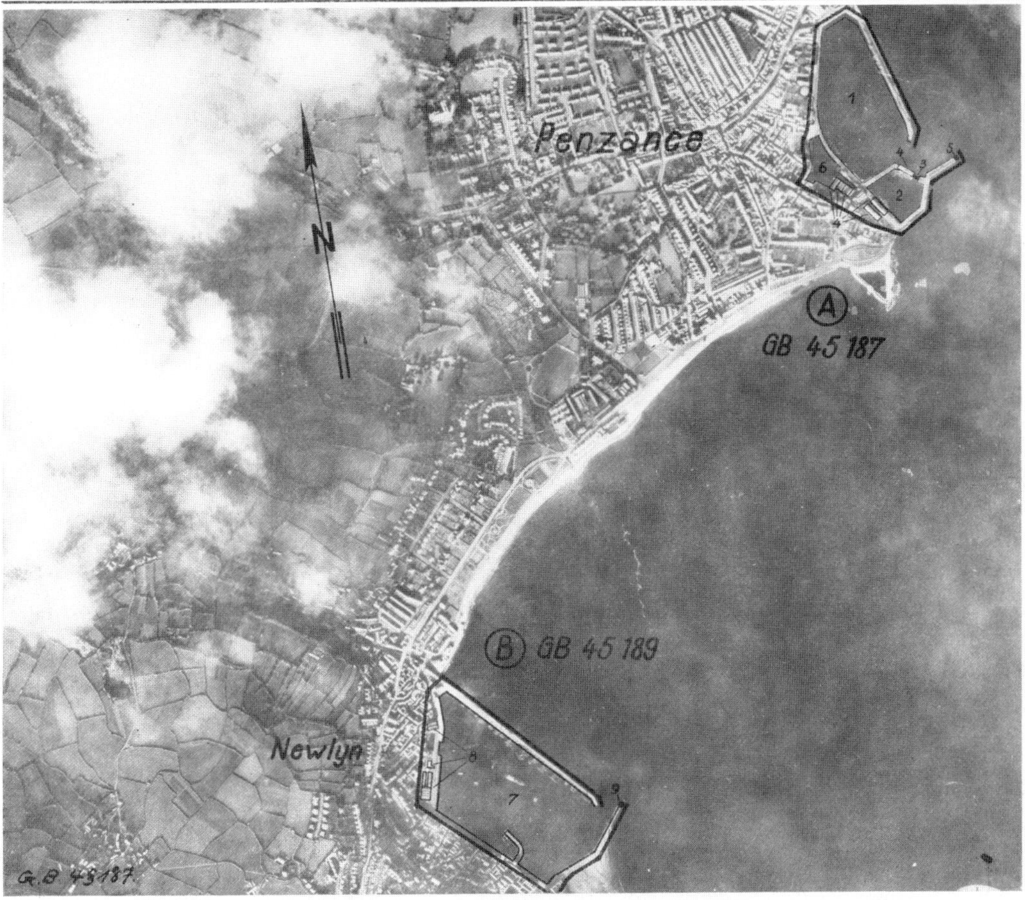

(A) GB 45 187 Hafenanlage

1) großes Hafenbecken, Kailänge ca 350 m
2) kleines Hafenbecken
3) Flutschleuse, Einfahrtsbreite ca 15 m
4) Lagergebäude etwa 4 000 qm
5) Leuchtfeuer
6) kleines Hafenbecken für Boote

(B) GB 45 189 Hafenanlage

7) Hafenbecken, Kailänge ca 500 m
8) Lagergebäude etwa 1 300 qm
9) Leuchtfeuer

Penzance
8th November 1940
Newlyn and Penzance Harbours
GB 45187

CORNWALL

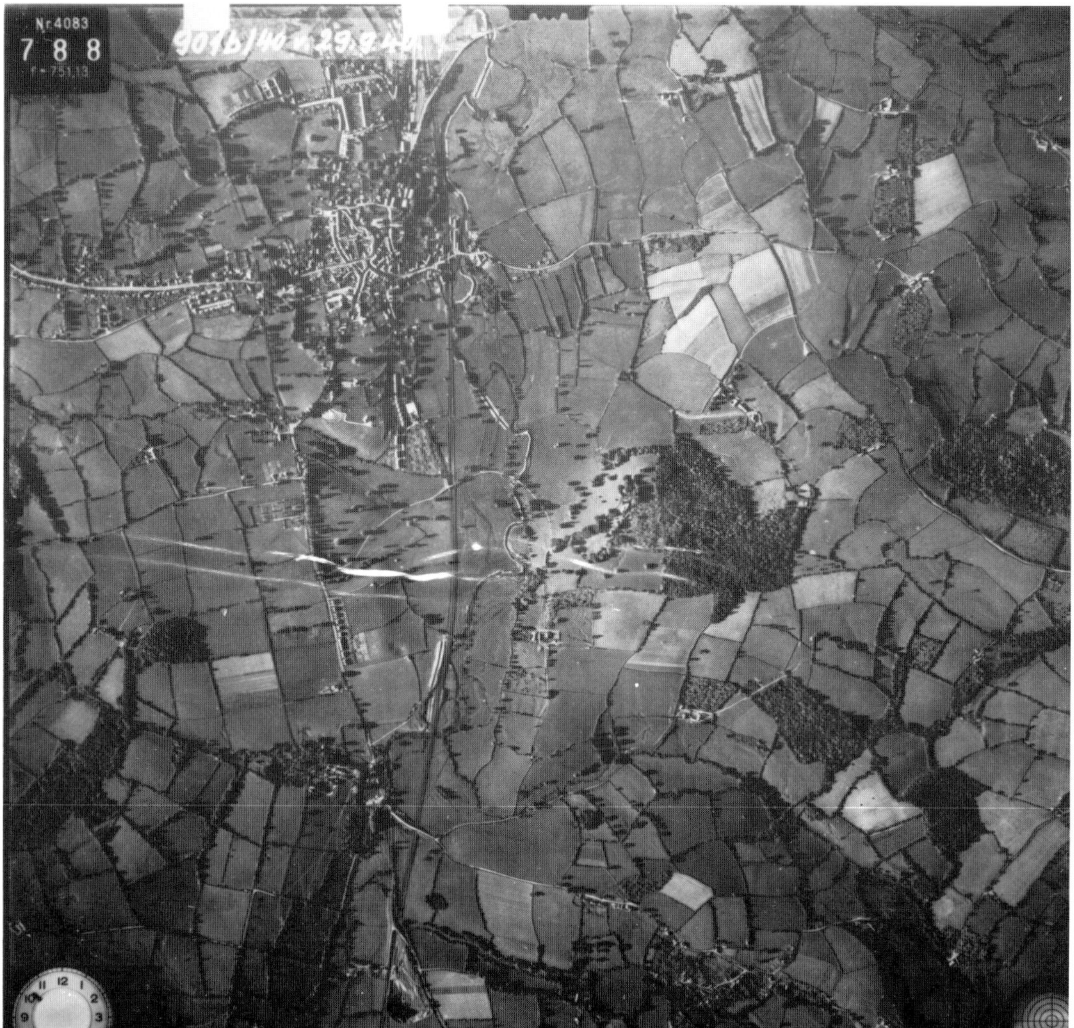

Axminster
29th September 1940
Axminster, Weycroft and Smallridge
GX 10313778

DEVON

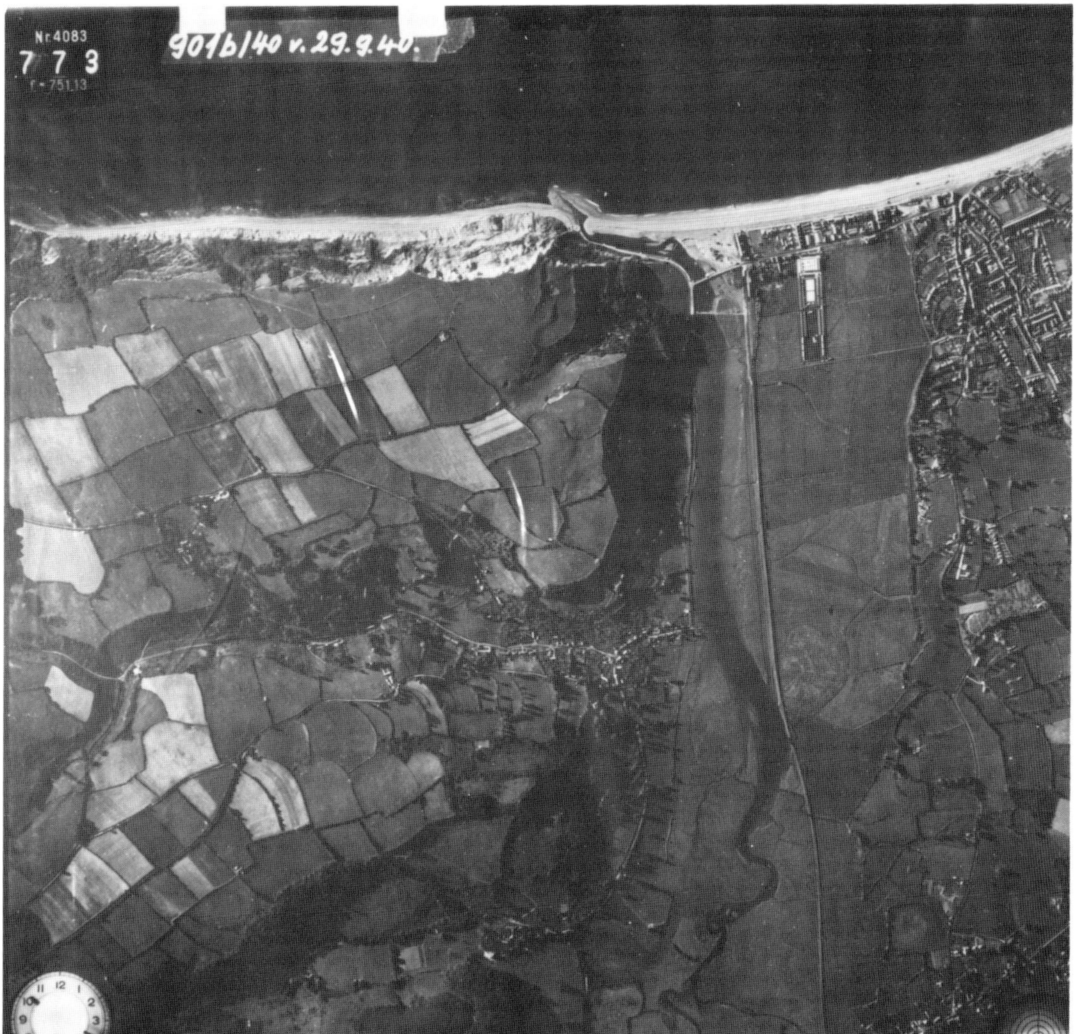

Axmouth
29th September 1940
Estuary of the River Axe
Seaton and village of Axmouth
GX 10313773
Comment
The Warners Holiday camp at Seaton was requisitioned as an internment camp for classified aliens. The Seaton internees included Jewish refugees and known Nazis. The camp was also used for Italian prisoners of war, and was eventually handed back to Warners after the war.

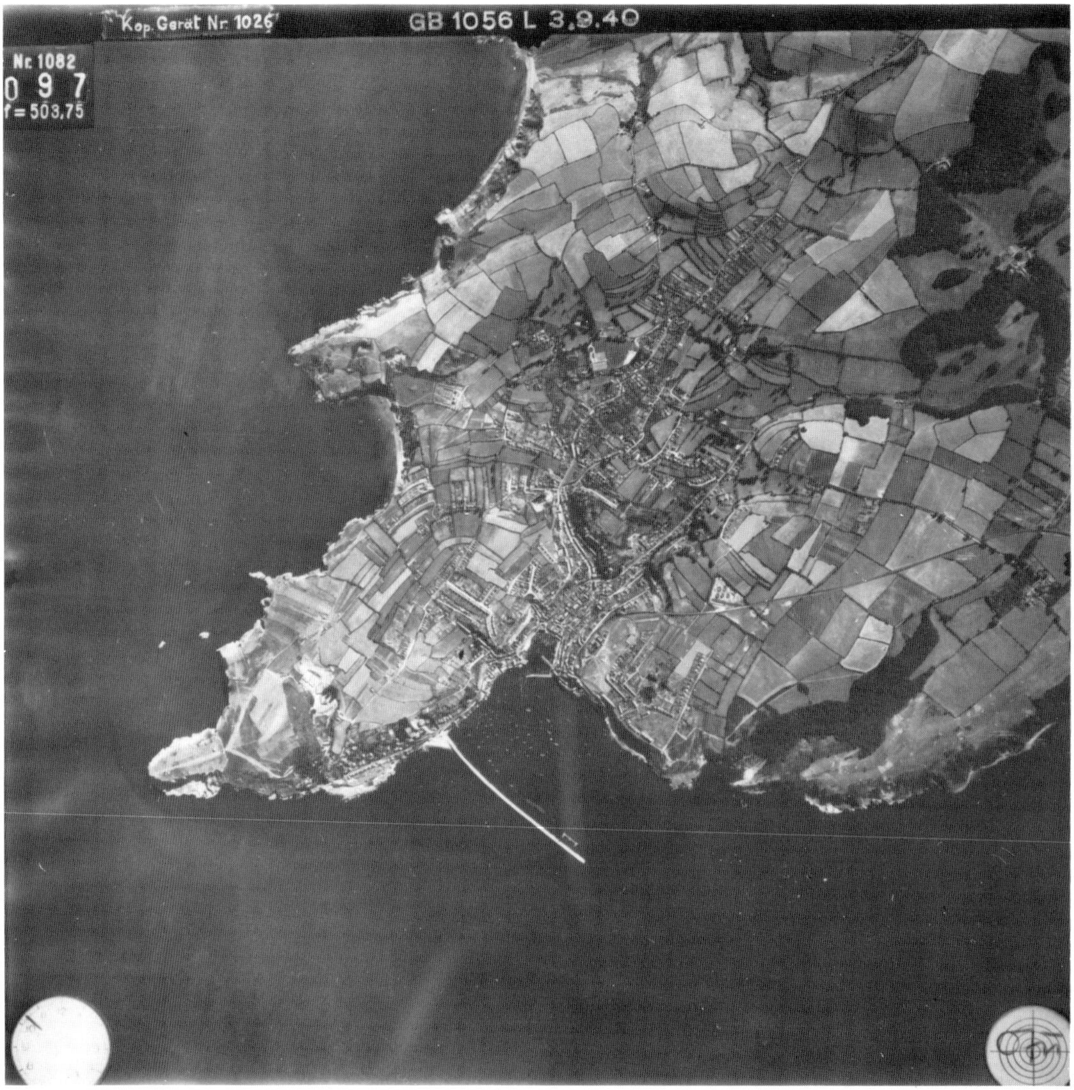

Brixham
3rd September 1940
Brixham and its hinterland
GX 103774097
Comment
The entrance to Brixham harbour was protected by two 4.7 inch naval guns and a minefield and boom were laid to protect the entrance. The fishing industry in Brixham, prior to the war had been in sharp decline with only six registered boats using the harbour in 1938.

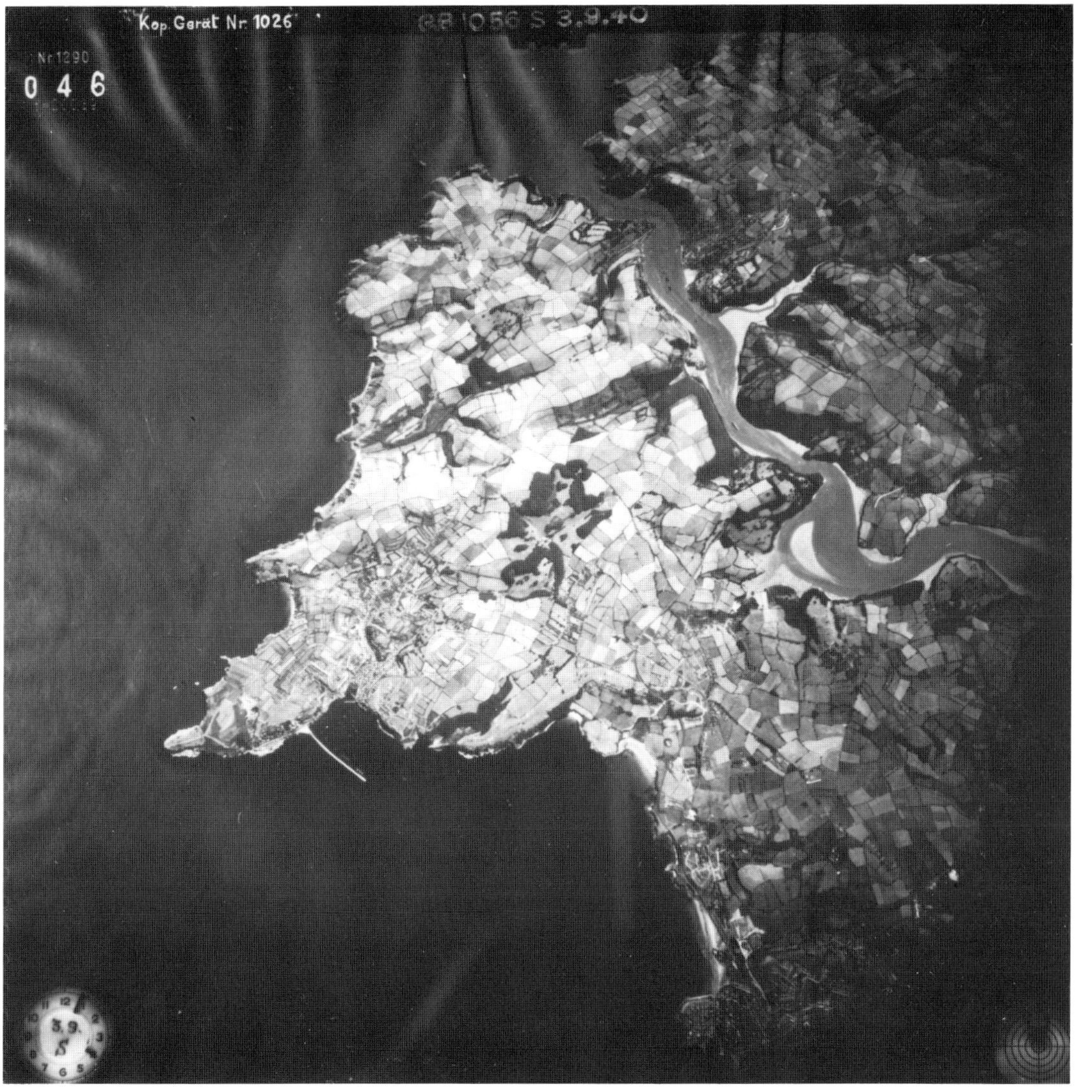

Brixham and Dartmouth
3rd September 1940
Brixham and the estuary of the River Dart
GX 10374047

GB 45 158 bc N. f. D.	Dartmouth Hafenanlage	Karte 1 : 100 000 Engl. Bl. 36 d

Bild Nr. F 914 b/006 Geogr. Lage 3°34'30" W 50°21' N, Höhe ü. d. M. 0 m Stand X.40

500 0 500 1000

Maßstab etwa 1: 16 500 (1 cm = 165 m) Lfl Kdo.3

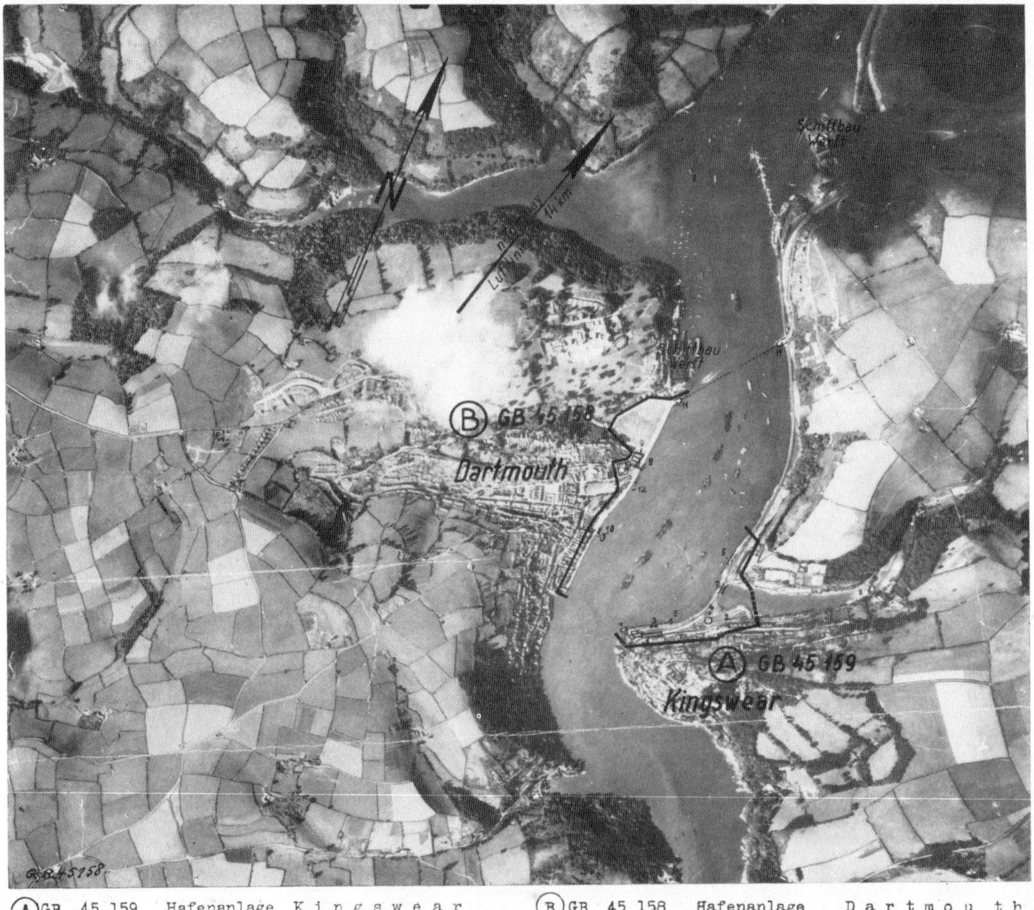

(A) GB 45 159 Hafenanlage Kingswear

1) Lager- und Umschlaghallen 1 120 qm
2) Umschlagplätze mit Gleisanschluß
3) 2 Krane fahrbar
4) Anlegesteg
5) Kaimauer, Länge 290 m
6) Drehscheibe
7) Eisenbahnbrücke.

(B) GB 45 158 Hafenanlage Dartmouth

8) Kohlenverladebrücke zum Gaswerk
9) 2 Hallen 1 000 qm
10) Anlegesteg
11) Anlegestellen der Dampffähre
12) Kaimauer, Länge 910 m.

Dartmouth
October 1940
Kingswear and Dartmouth
GB 45158
Comment
In 1938 the local Council decided that Dartmouth would not be considered a target by the Luftwaffe. At the outbreak of war the local population were to be informed of an air raid by the sounding of a steam whistle at the local gas works. The population of Dartmouth in 1938 was 6,000.

GB 45 163 b c | **Exeter** | Karte 1 : 100 000
N. f. D. | Hafen | Engl. Bl. 36 b

Bild Nr. 278 Z 40 **Geogr. Lage** 3°32′ W, 50°43′ N, **Höhe ü. d. M.** 30 m **Stand** XI. 40.

Maßstab etwa 1 : 13 500 (1 cm = 135 m) Lfl. Kdo. 3.

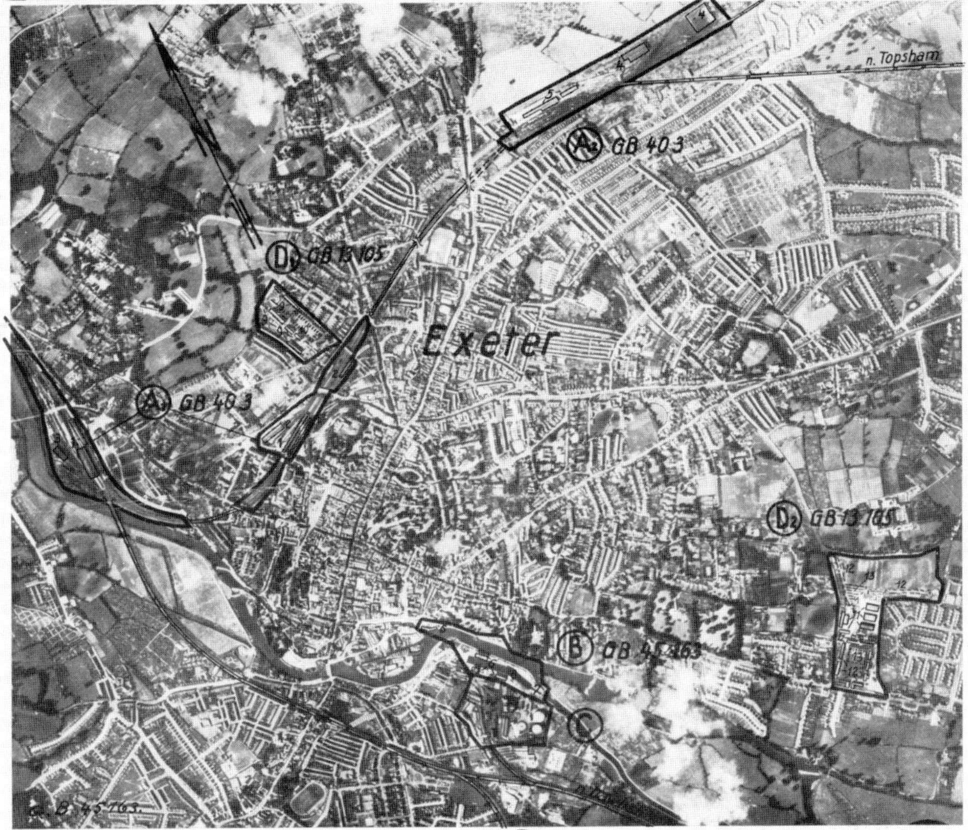

(A1) GB 40 3 Bahnhof

1) Bahnhofsgebäude und Bahnsteigüberdachungen	etwa	7 000 qm
2) Güterhallen	etwa	3 000 qm
3) Lokschuppen	etwa	700 qm
bebaute Fläche	etwa	10 700 qm
Gesamtfläche	etwa	150 000 qm

(A2)

4) Werkstatthallen	etwa	13 000 qm
5) Lagergebäude	etwa	3 500 qm
bebaute Fläche	etwa	16 500 qm
Gesamtfläche	etwa	160 000 qm

(B) GB 45 163 Hafen

6) Lagergebäude	etwa	2 200 qm
7) 2 Schleusen		
8) Hafenbecken		

Kailänge etwa 1 100 m

(C) Gaswerk

(D1) GB 13 105 Kasernen

9) 7 Kasernengebäude	etwa	5 000 qm
10) 15 Unterkunftsbaracken	etwa	1 000 qm
bebaute Fläche	etwa	6 000 qm
Gesamtfläche	etwa	46 000 qm

(D2)

11) 6 Lagerhallen	etwa	4 000 qm
12) 15 Kasernengebäude	etwa	4 500 qm
13) 30 Unterkunftsbaracken	etwa	7 000 qm
bebaute Fläche	etwa	15 500 qm
Gesamtfläche	etwa	130 000 qm

Exeter
November 1940
Barracks and Gas Works
GB 45163
Comment
On 24th April 1942, sixty German bombers attacked and heavily bombed the city causing massive destruction. The attack was one of a number known as the 'Baedeker Raids' by the Luftwaffe on selected historical English towns, in retaliation for similar raids by the RAF on German cities. During the five days of the 'Baedeker Raids' over nine hundred civilians were killed. It was only due to heavy losses the Luftwaffe suffered, that the raids were stopped.

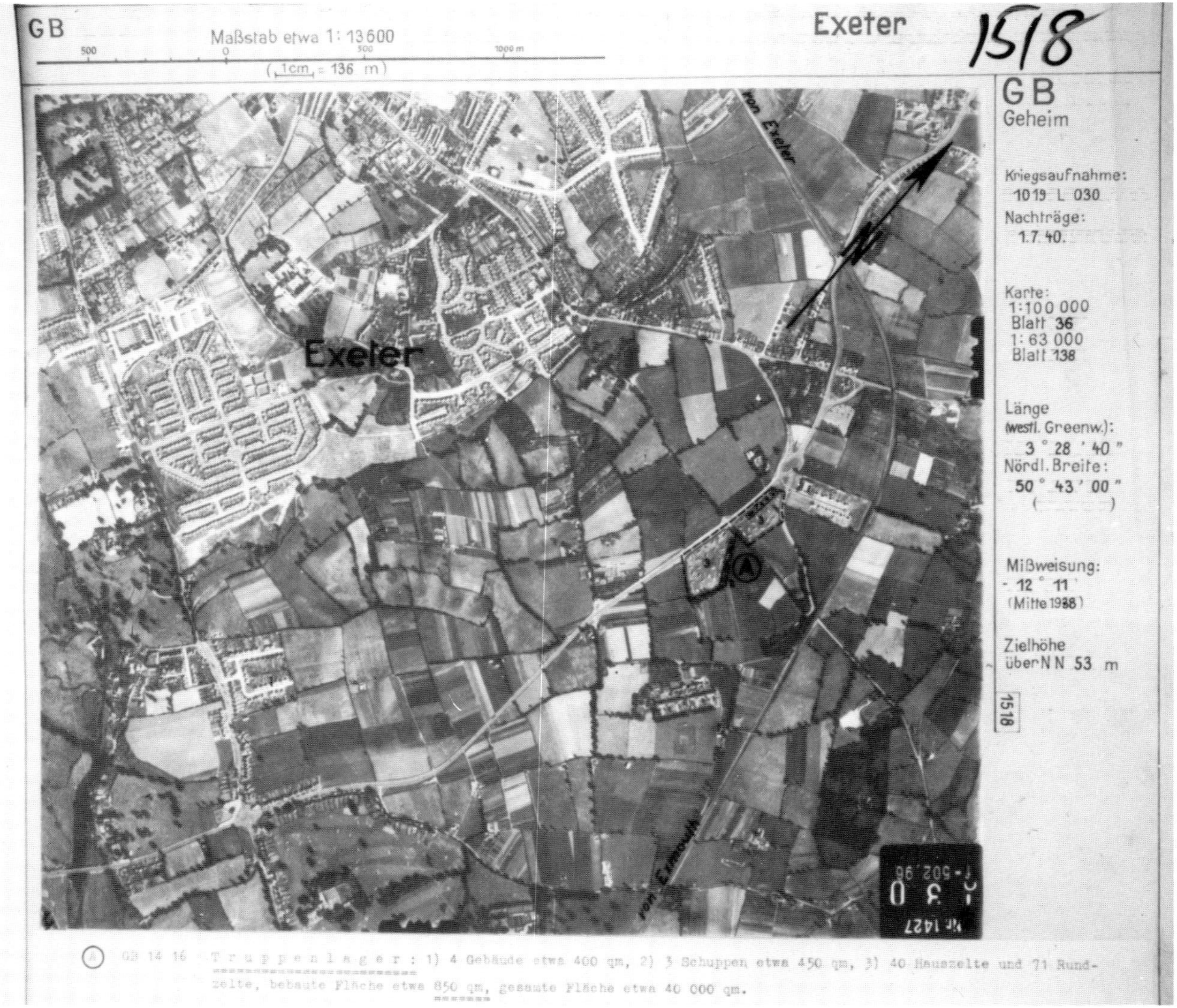

Exeter
1st July 1940
Wireless Station
TN 1518

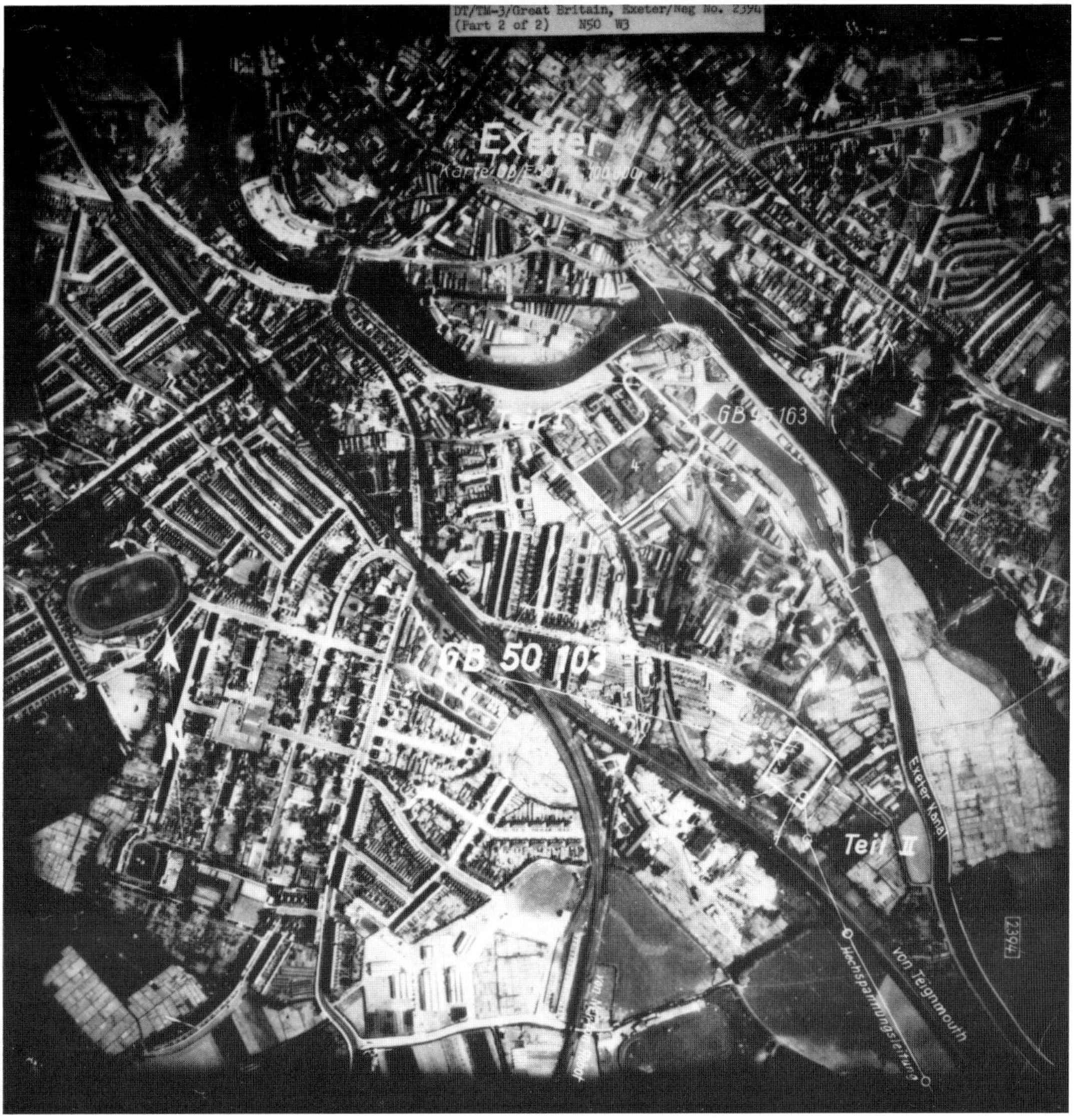

Exeter
3rd September 1940
Power Station
TN 2394
Comment
Exeter was described as the 'Jewel in the West'. The old timbered buildings narrow passages and alleyways of Devon's county town burnt easily and suffered great damage during the blitz.

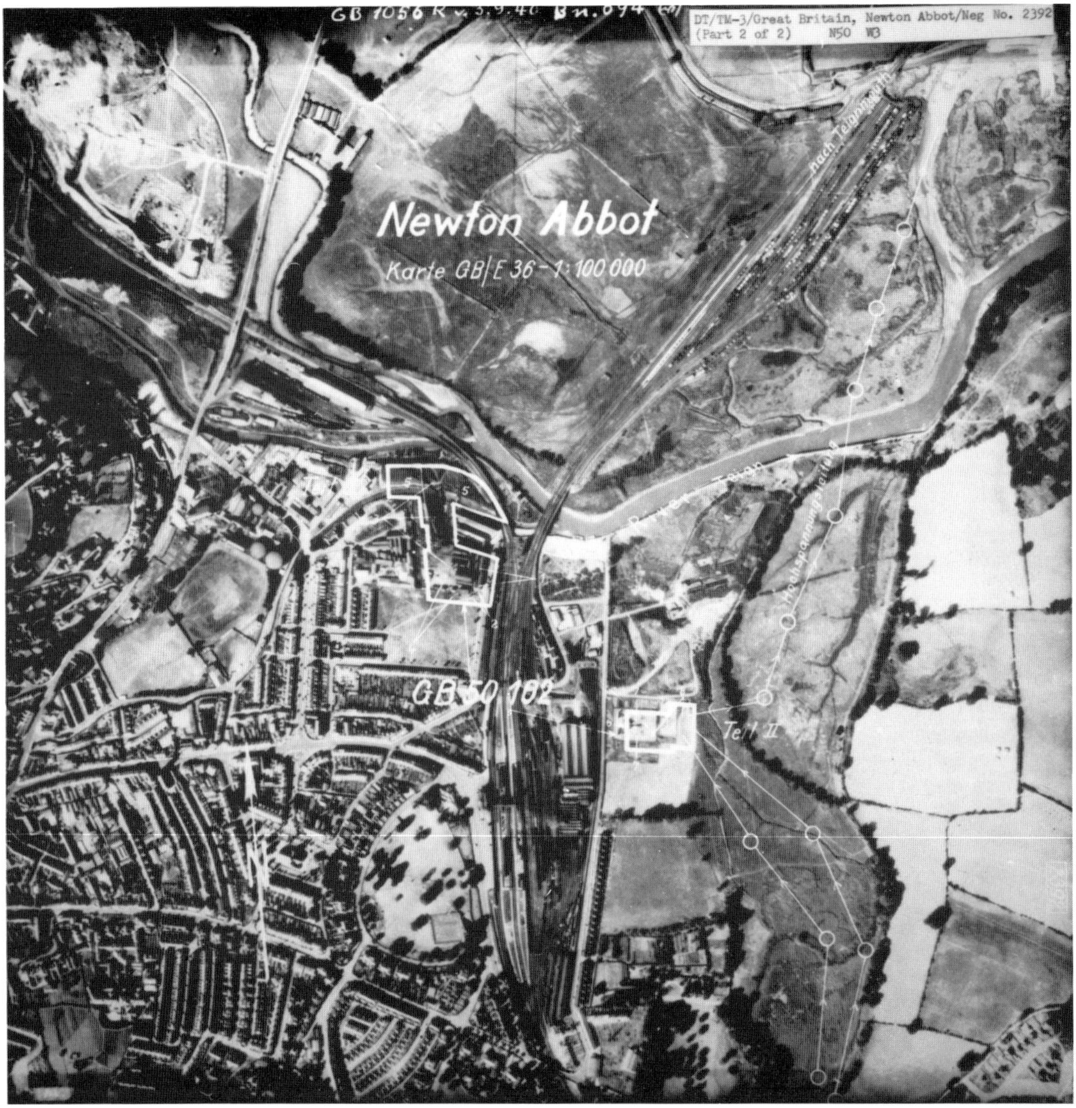

Newton Abbot
3rd September 1940
Power Station and Railway Station
TN 2392
Comment
The railway station was bombed on the 20th August 1940 by three planes, killing three people.

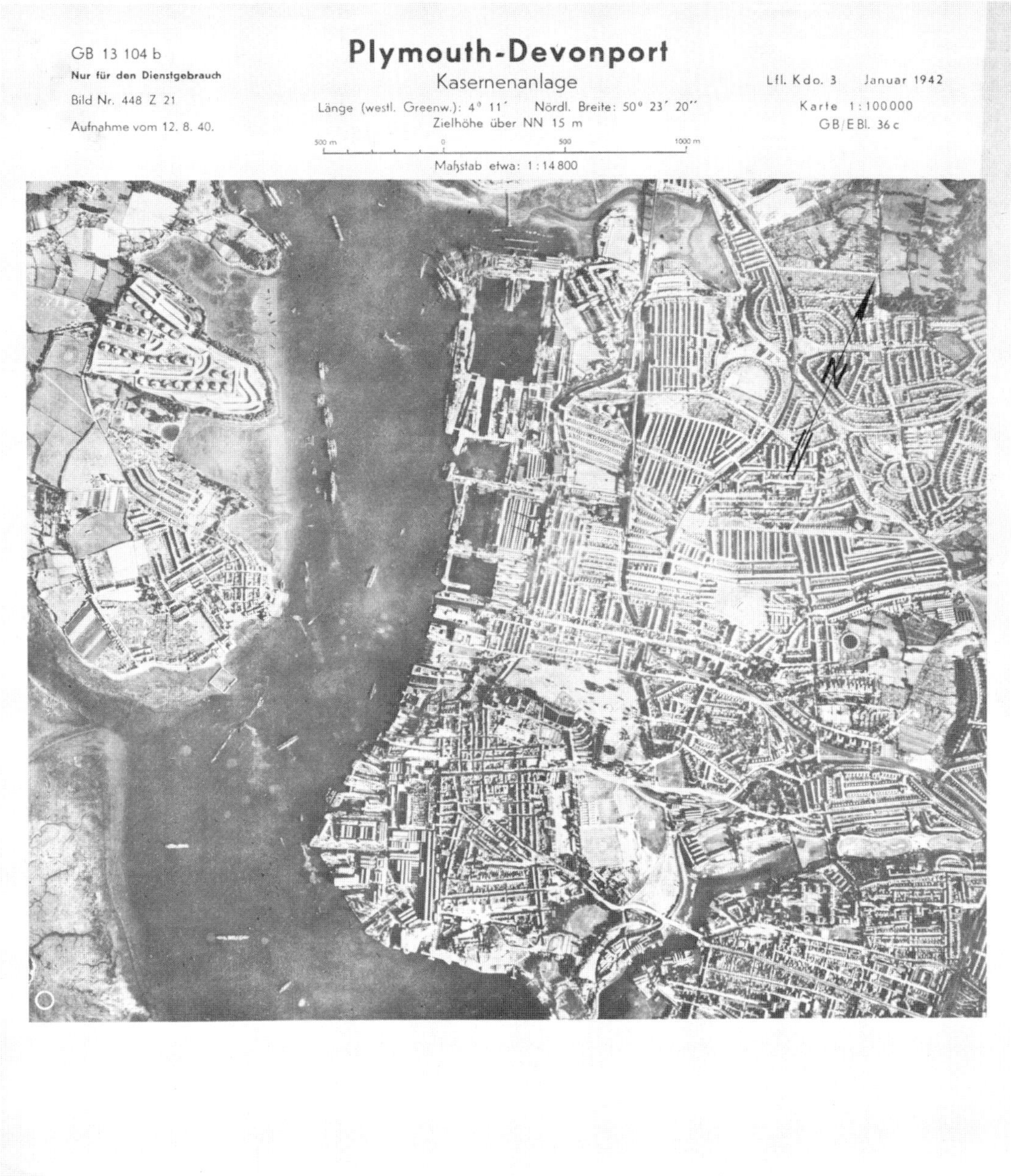

Plymouth
3rd January 1942
Devonport, Royal Naval Docks and Shipyards
GB 13104 B

GB 49 69 bc
N. f. D.

Plymouth-Crownhill
Sendeanlage

Karte 1:100000
Engl.Bl. 36c

Bild Nr. 462 Z 10 **Geogr. Lage** 4°09' W, 50° 25' N, **Höhe ü. d. M.** 60 m **Stand** X. 40

Lfl. Kdo. 3

Maßstab etwa 1: 14 500 (1 cm 145 m)

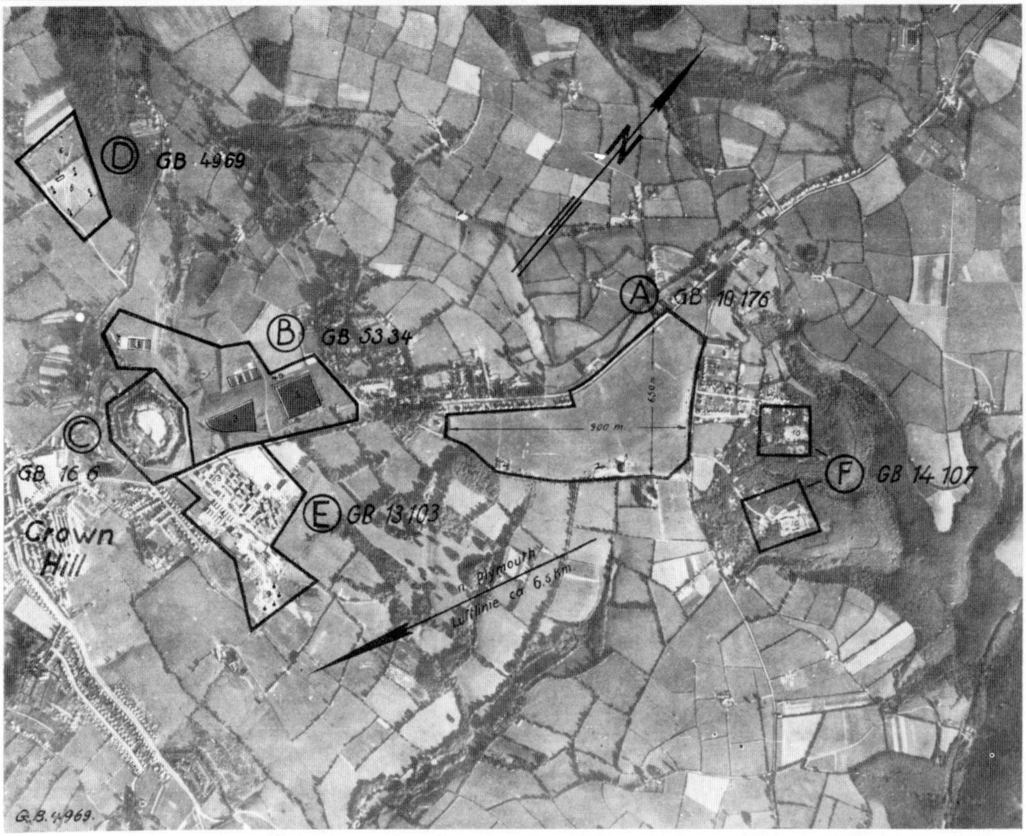

(A) GB 10 176 Flugplatz 650 x 900 m
1) 1 Halle etwa 300 qm
2) Nebengebäude etwa 1 000 qm
bebaute Fläche etwa 1 300 qm

(B) GB 53 34 Wasserwerk
3) Filteranlagen
4) Pumpenhäuser etwa 240 qm
Gesamtfläche etwa 220 000 qm

(C) GB 16 6 Fort Crownhill

(D) GB 49 69 Sendeanlage Crownhill
6) 7 Sendemasten (3 im Bau)
7) Betriebsgebäude etwa 400 qm

(E) GB 13 103 Kasernenanlage Crownhill
8) Unterkunfts- und Nebengebäude, Baracken etwa 14 100 qm
9) schwere Flakstellung
Gesamte Fläche etwa 180 000 qm

(F) GB 14 107 Zeltlager Woolwell
10) Südteil: 1 Halle, 2 Baracken, 51 Hauszelte, ~~10 Rundzelte~~ etwa 2 400 qm
Nordteil: ~~53 Rundzelte~~
Gesamte Fläche etwa 27 000 qm

Plymouth-Crownhill
1940
Airfield, Waterworks and Barracks
GB 4969

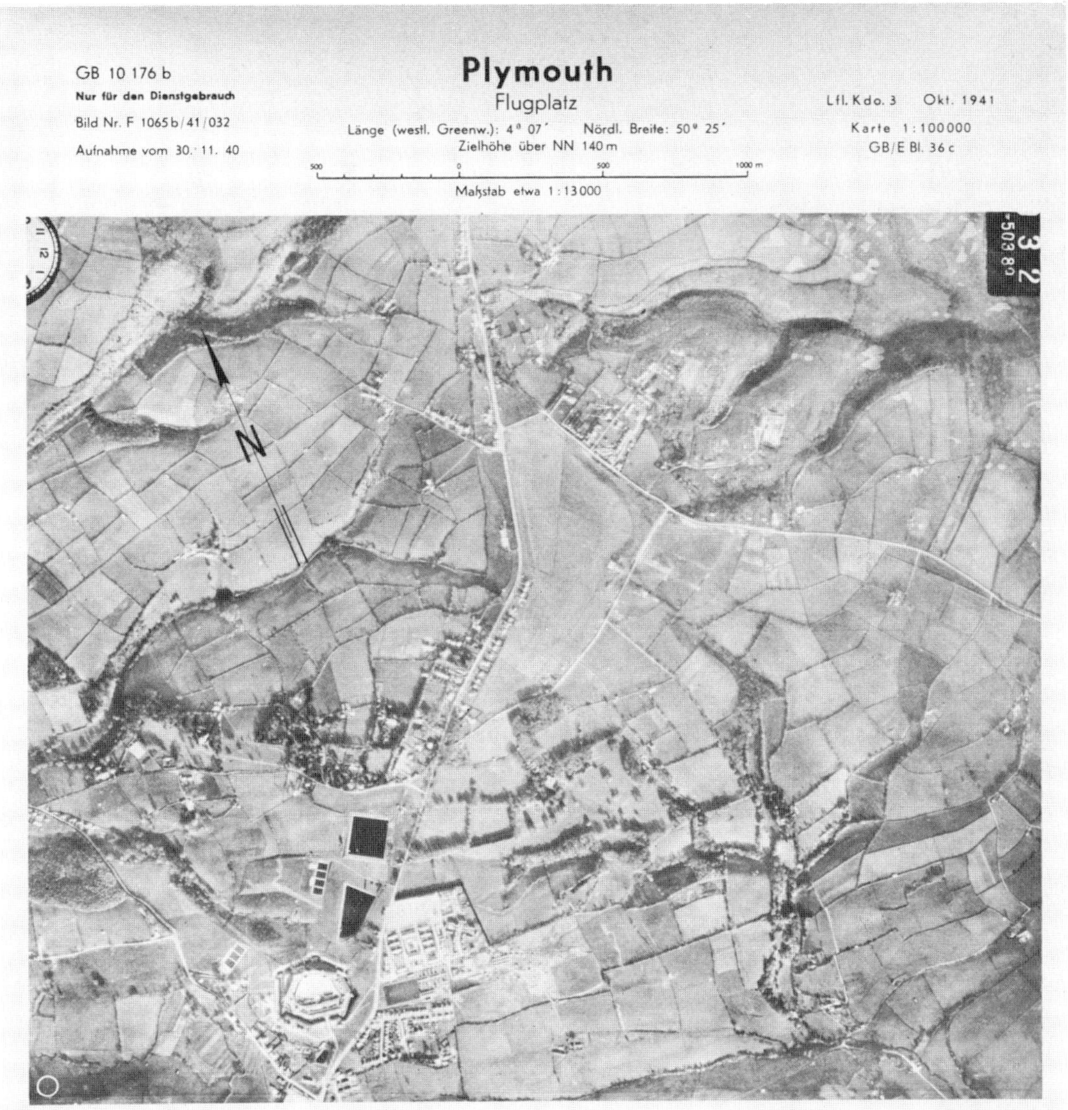

Plymouth
October 1941
Airfield
GB 10176

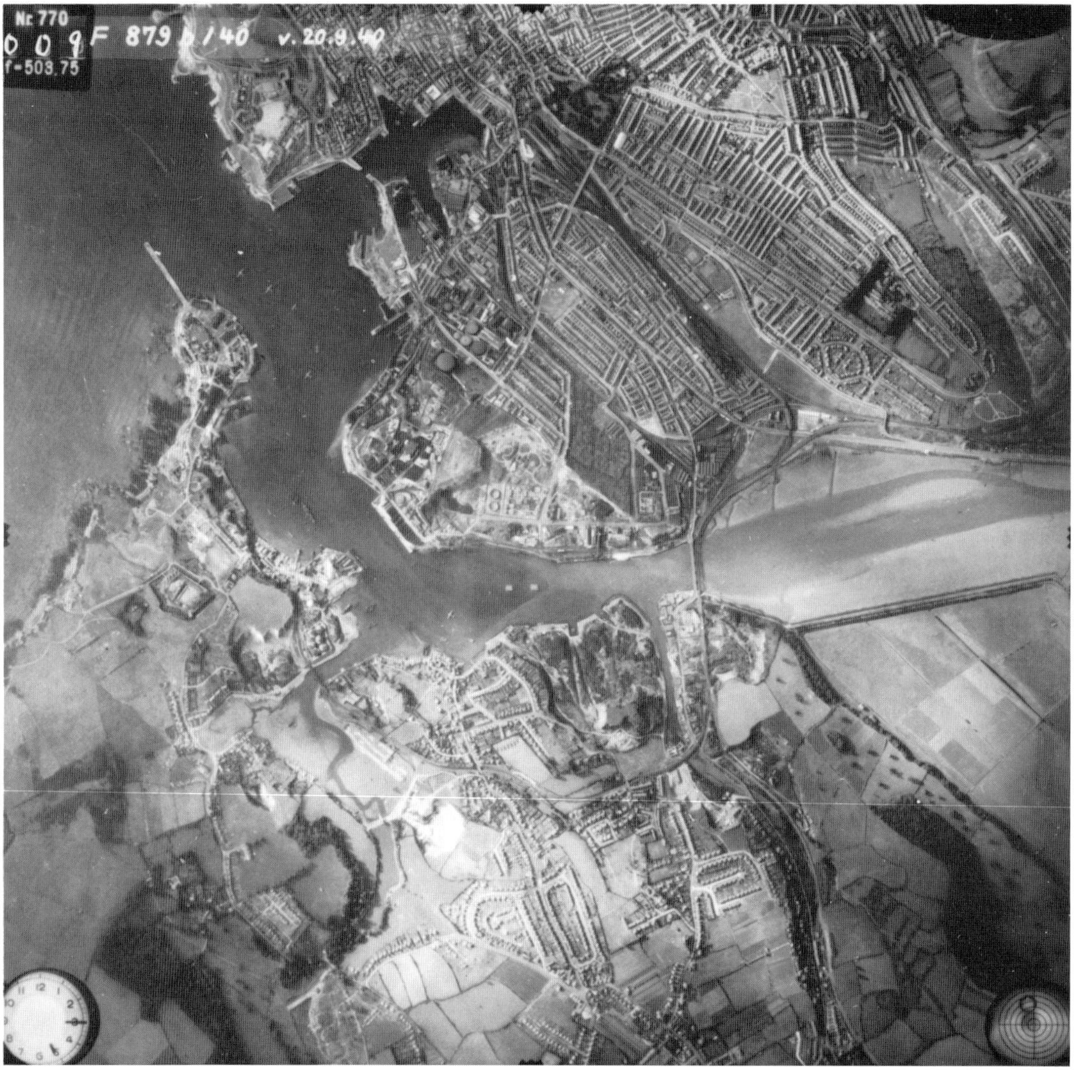

Plymouth
20th September 1940
Plymstock, Mountbatten and Plymouth Hoe
GX 10335 009

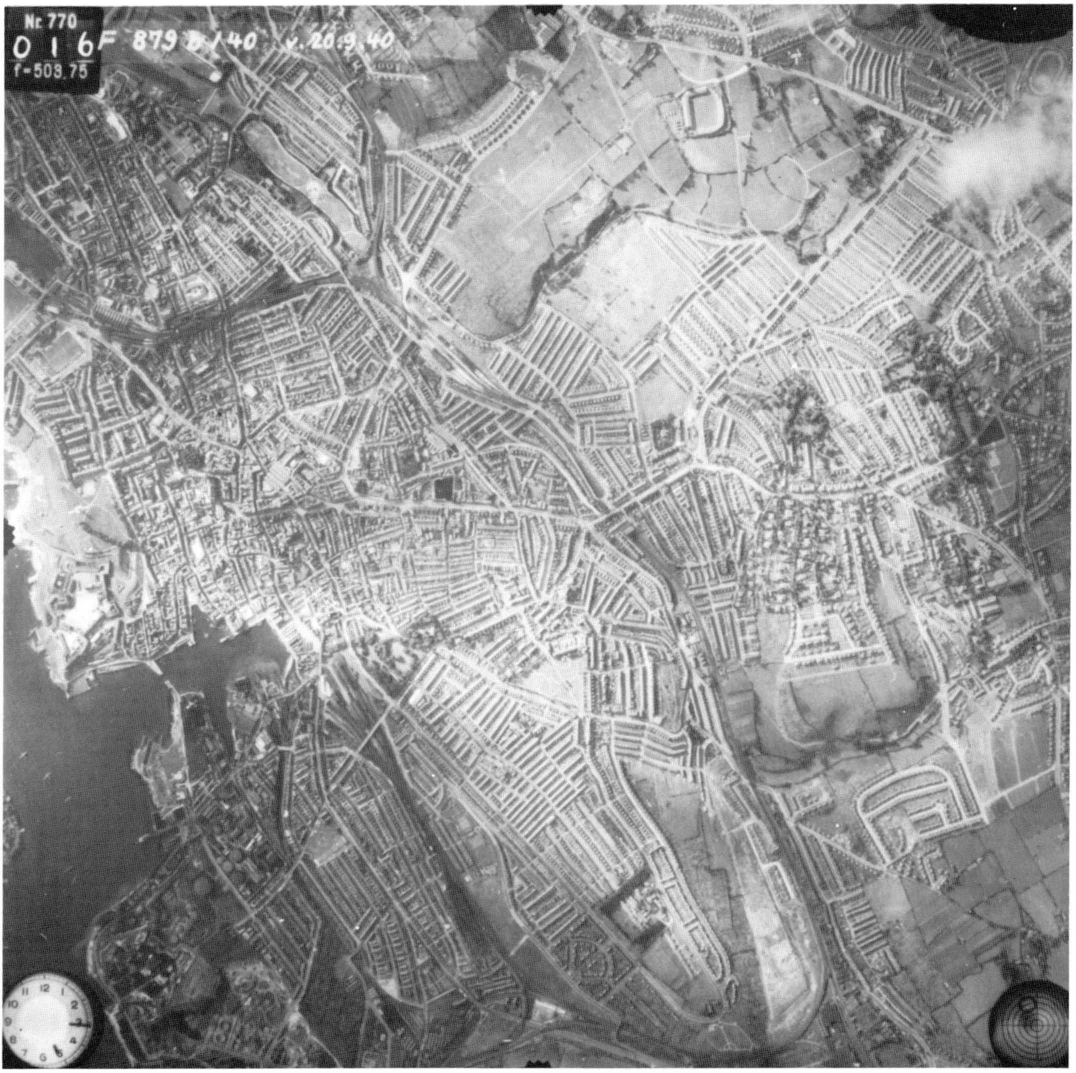

Plymouth
20th September 1940
Stonehouse and The Barbican
GX 10335 016
Comment
The first recorded attack on Plymouth was on 27th November 1940. A force of 112 bombers over a period of 8 hours dropped 100 tons of bombs and 6,000 incendiary bombs. The main target was RAF Mountbatten, where the Luftwaffe destroyed a hangar and two planes. From November 1940 to April 1941 the Luftwaffe dropped over 260,000 incendiaries on Plymouth. The city centre was destroyed as was the Guildhall and numerous other buildings. The city suffered some of the greatest damage in the United Kingdom, which during the war went largely unreported due to the strict censorship of news.

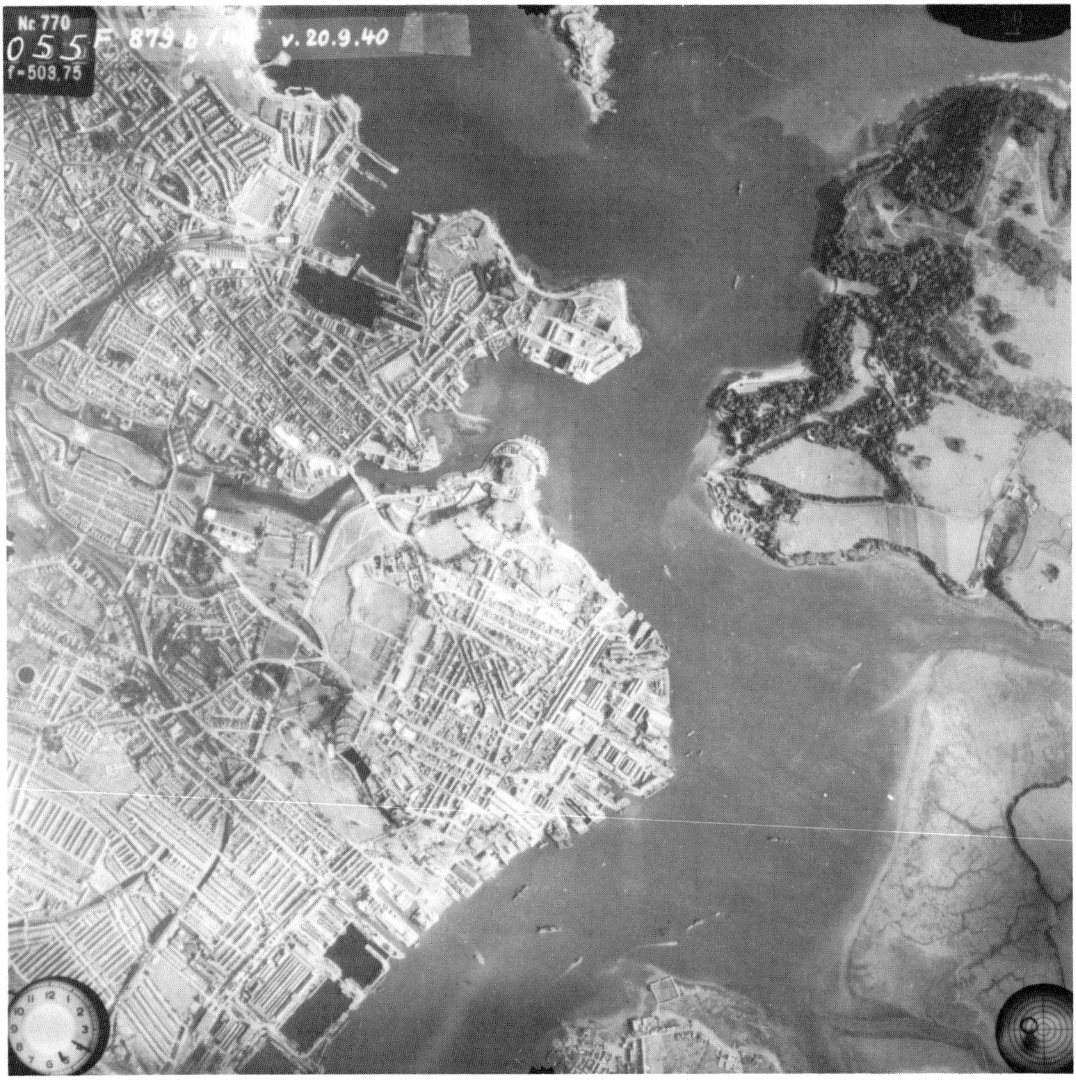

Plymouth
20th September 1940
Stonehouse, Mount Wise and Mount Edgecumbe
GX 10335 055

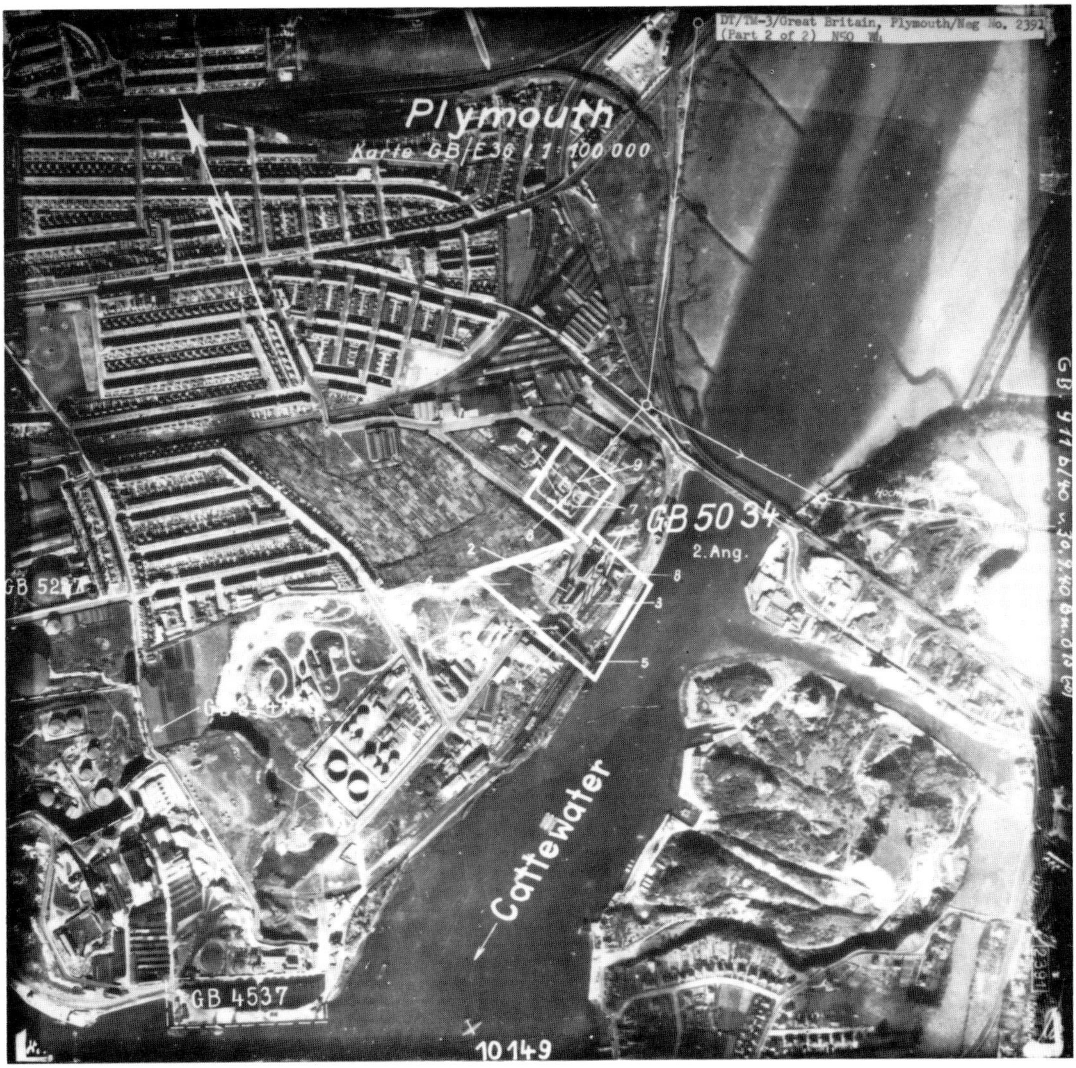

Plymouth
12th August 1940
Devonport
TN 2391

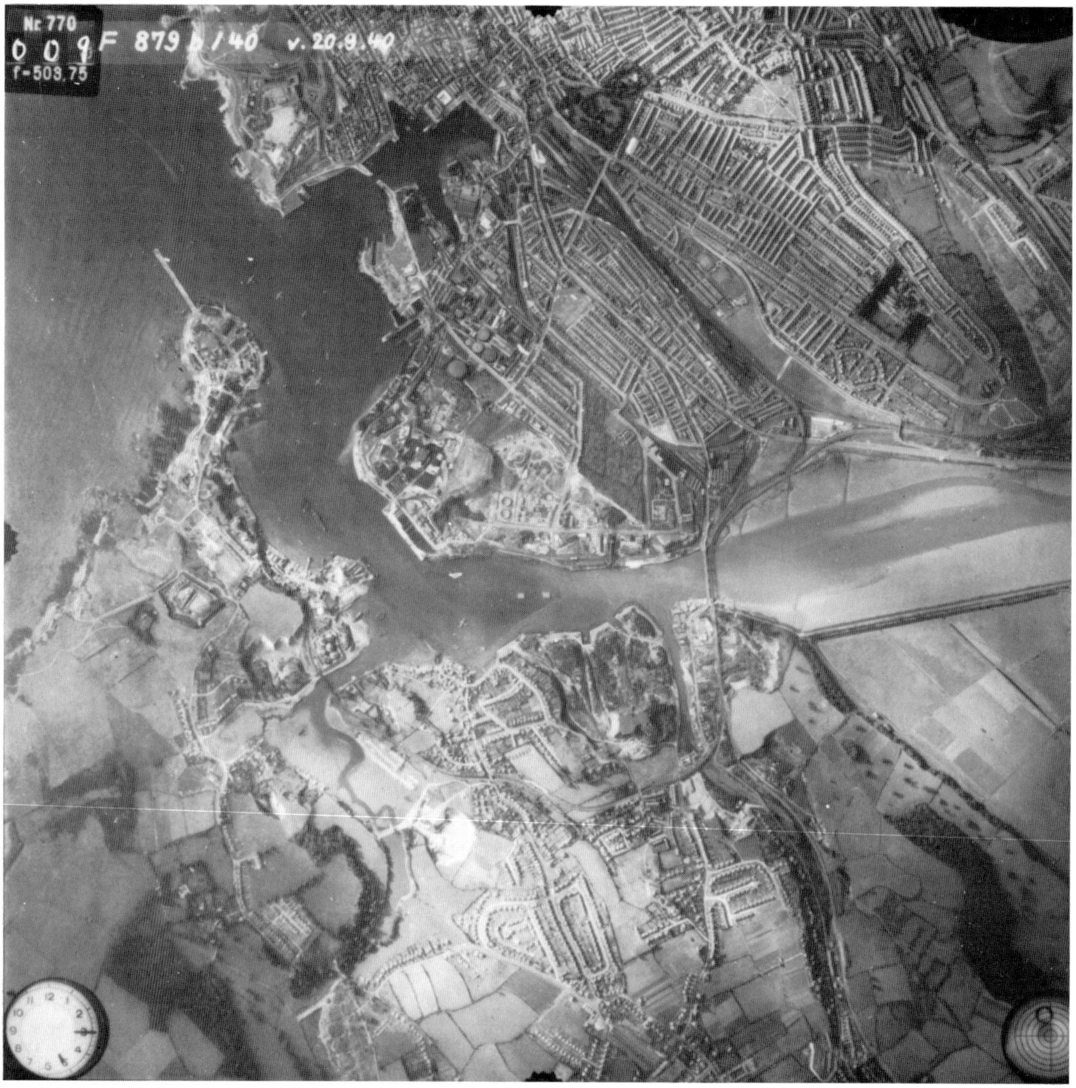

Plymouth
20th September 1940
Landulph, Cargreen and Warl Point
GX 10335 051

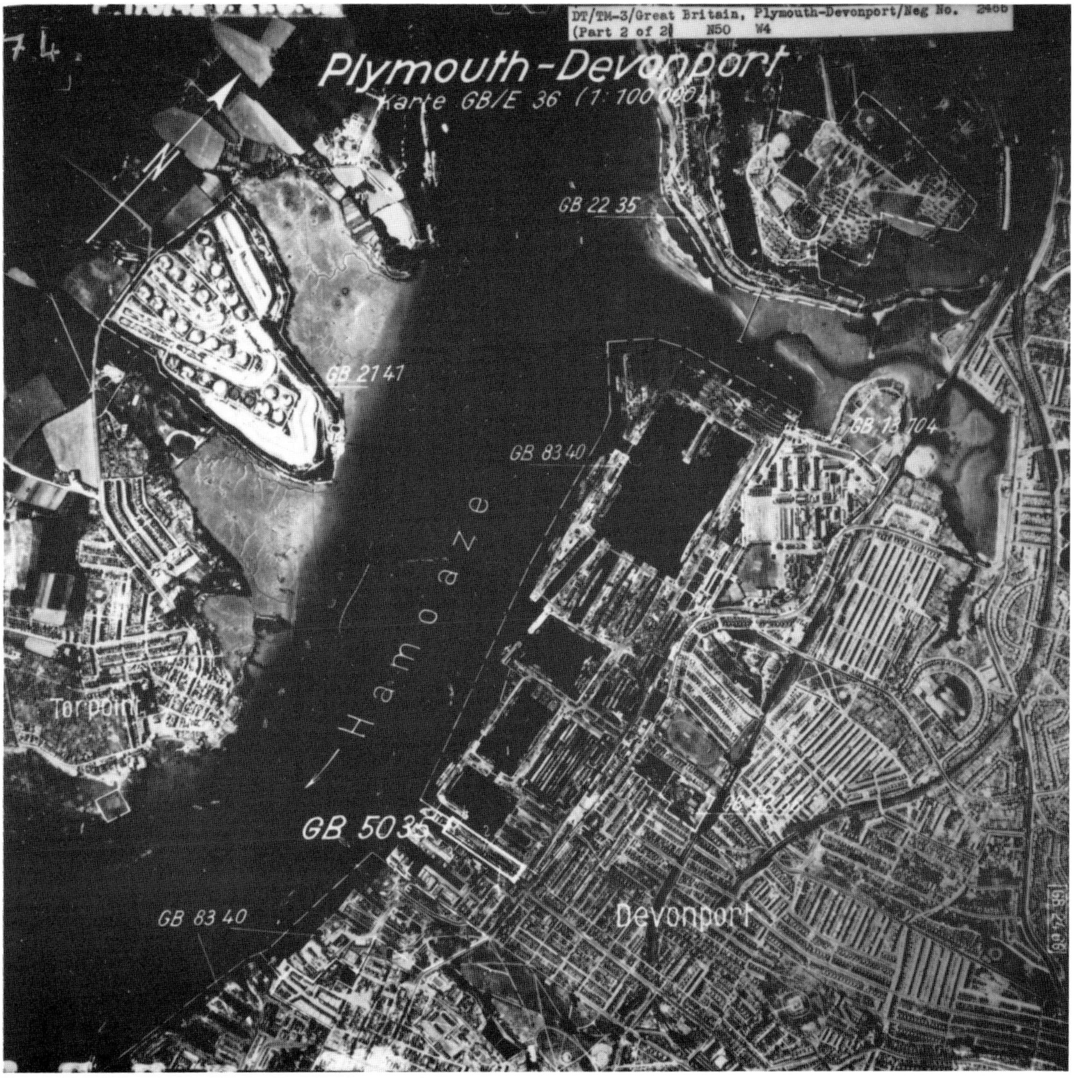

Plymouth
21st June 1942
Devonport Docks
TN 2466

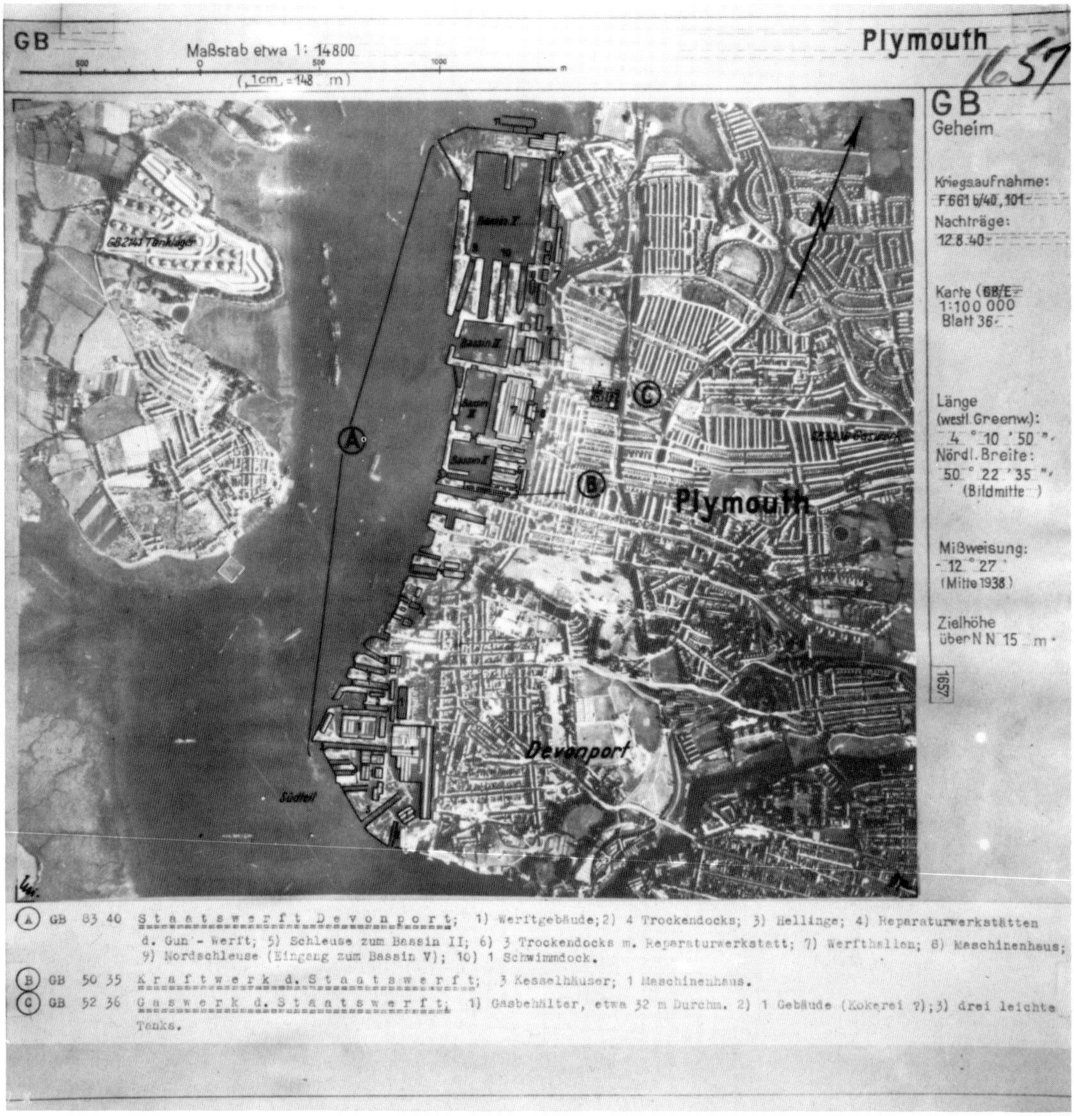

Plymouth
12th August 1940
Devonport
TN 1657

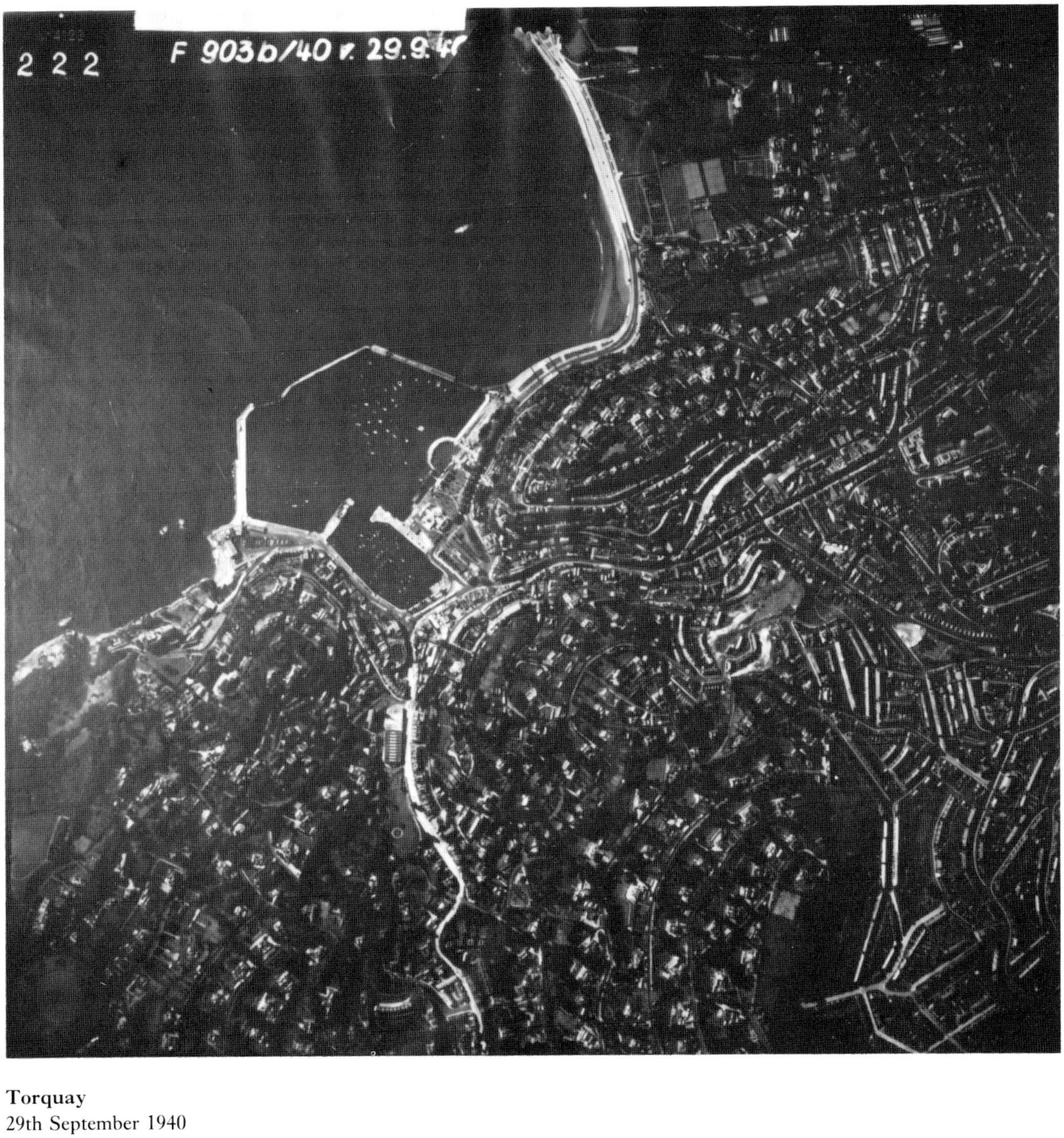

Torquay
29th September 1940
Torquay town and harbour
GX 10318 222
Comment
The harbour at Torquay was protected at the outbreak of war by the sinking of two block ships and the placing of torpedo launchers near the entrance.

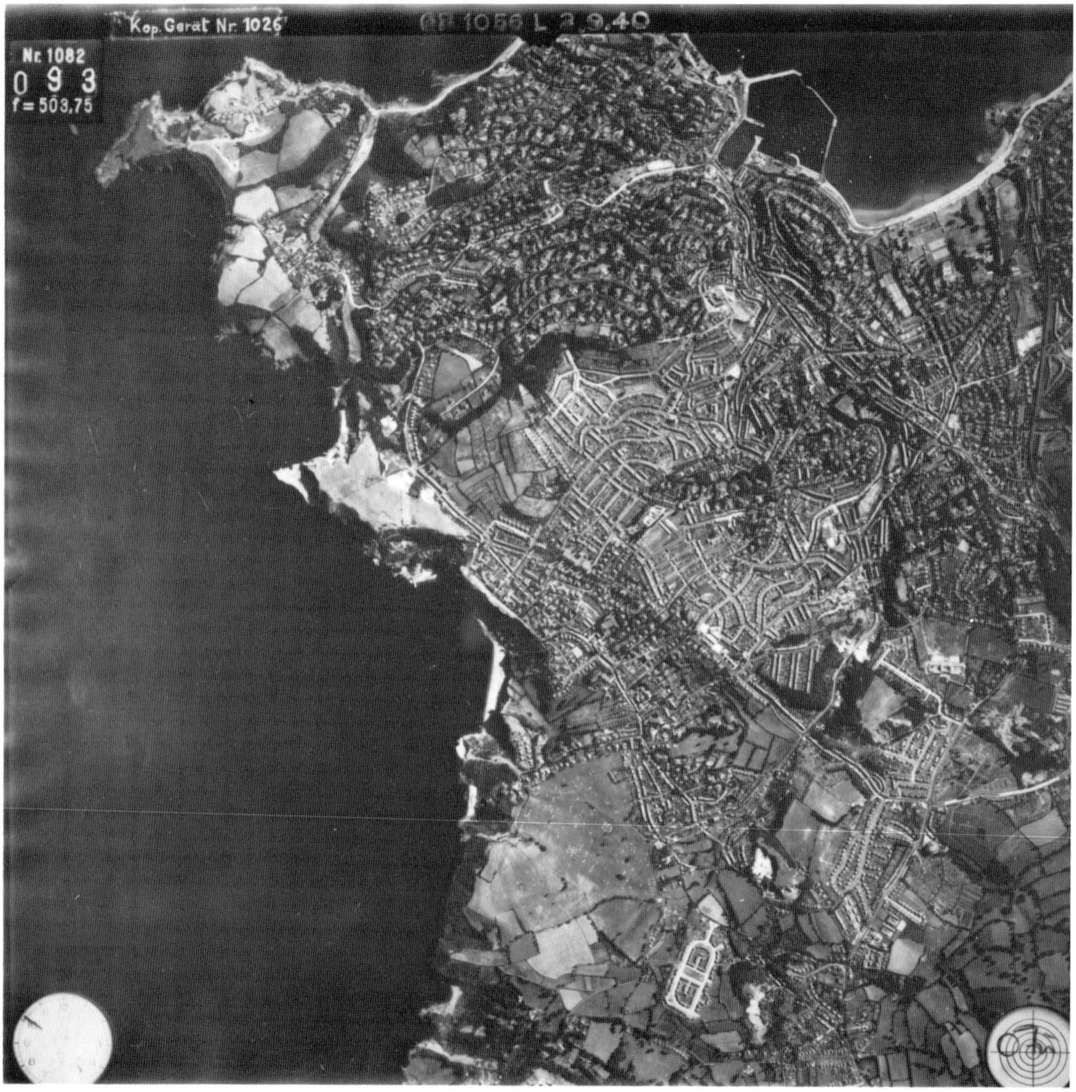

Torquay
3rd September 1940
Torquay
GX 10374 093

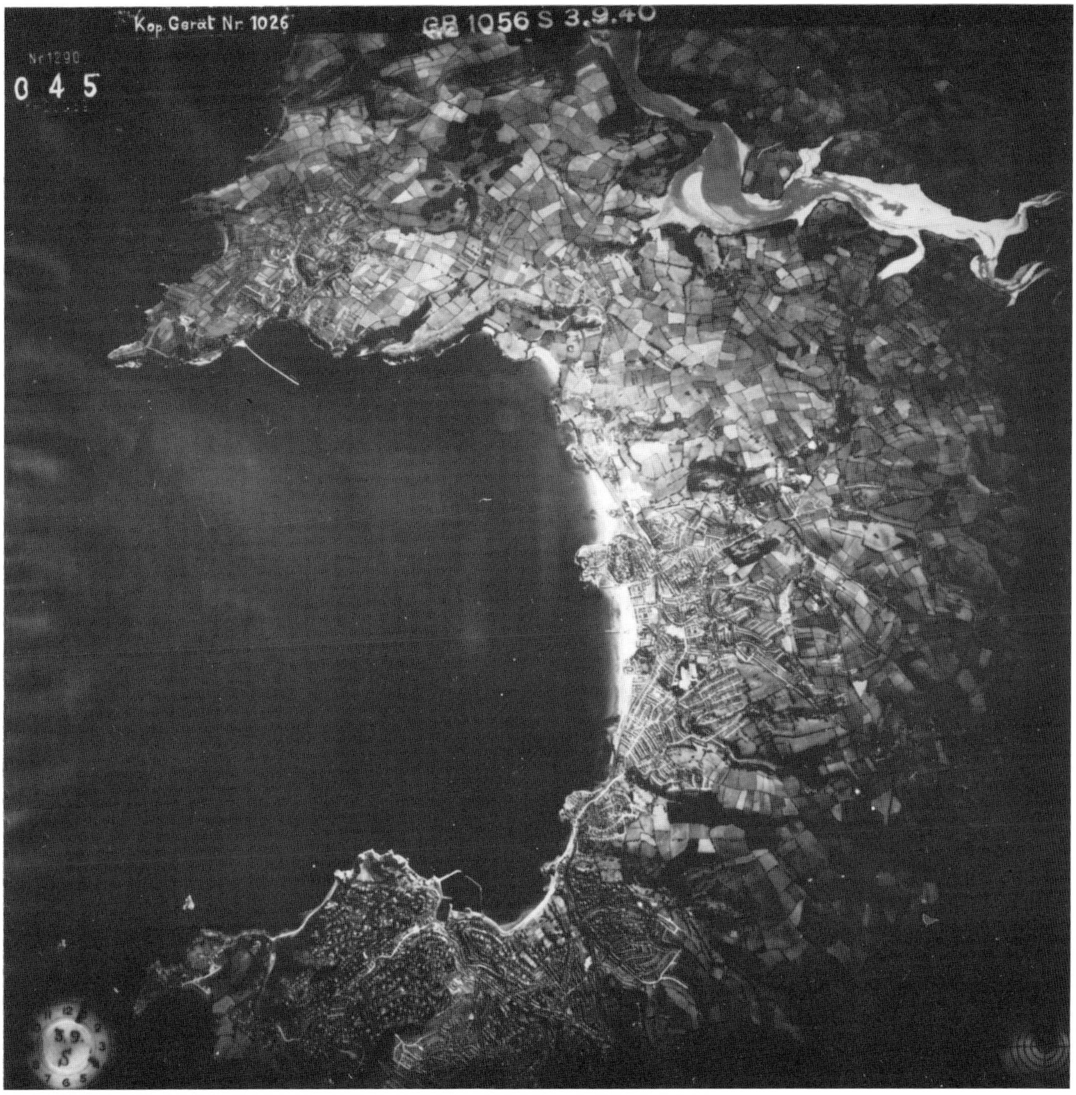

Torbay
3rd September 1940
Torbay, Torquay and Brixham
GX 10374 045

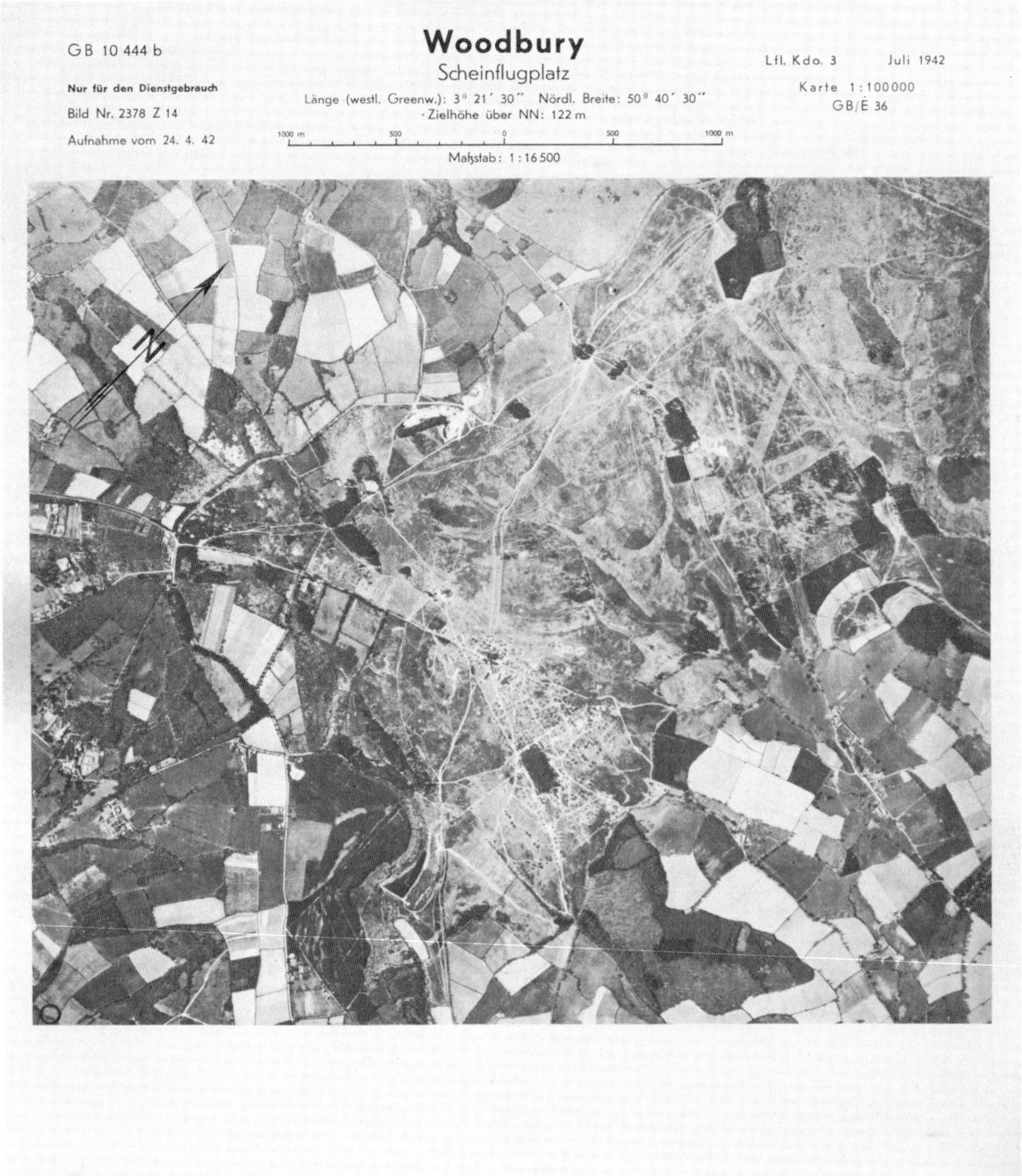

Woodbury
24th April 1942
Woodbury Common
GB 10444
Comment
During the war Woodbury was used as a dummy airfield, and landing lights were laid out to attract the German bombers away from their intended targets.

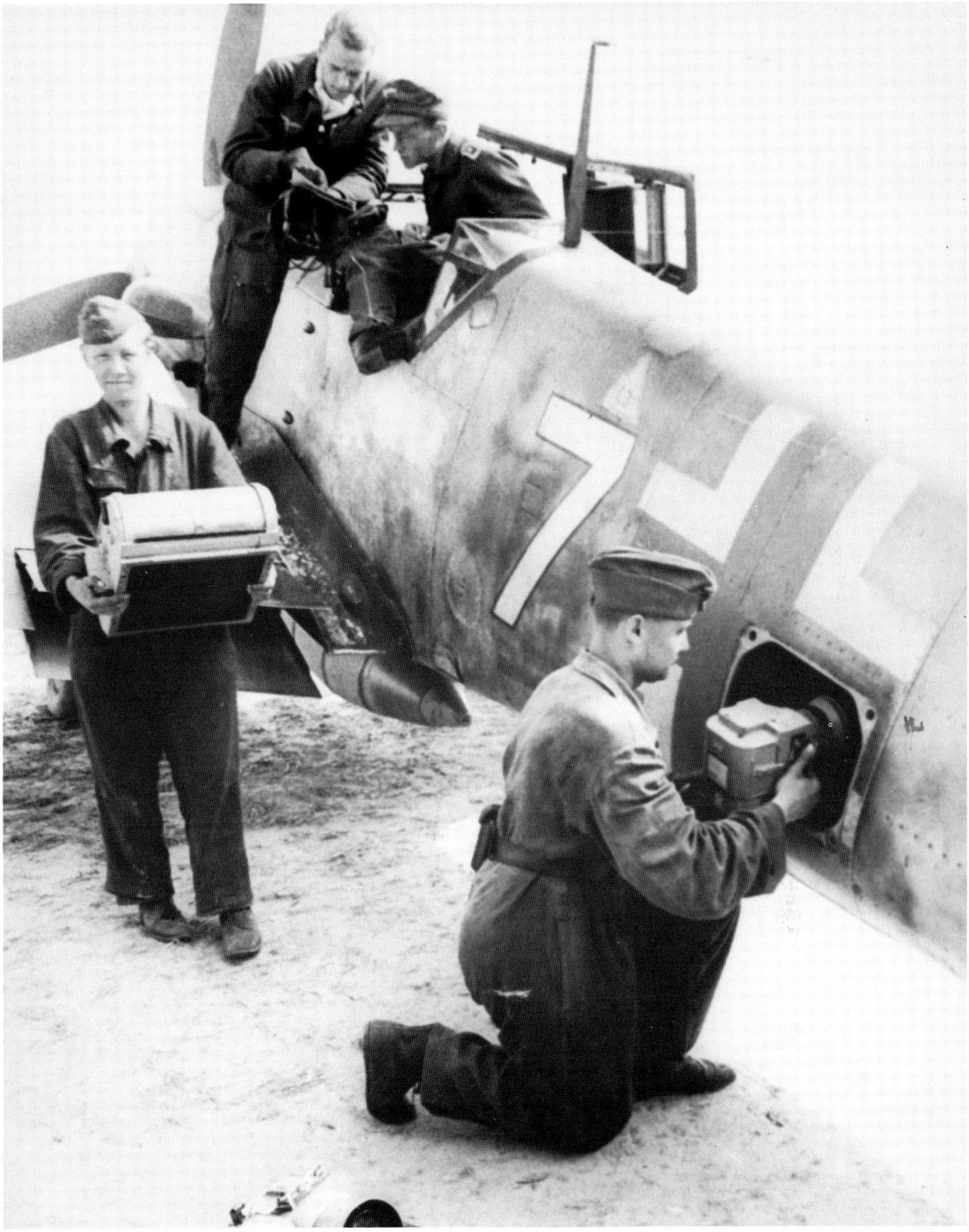

A Luftwaffe technician slides the camera onto the port side of a reconnaissance version of the Messerschmitt 109.

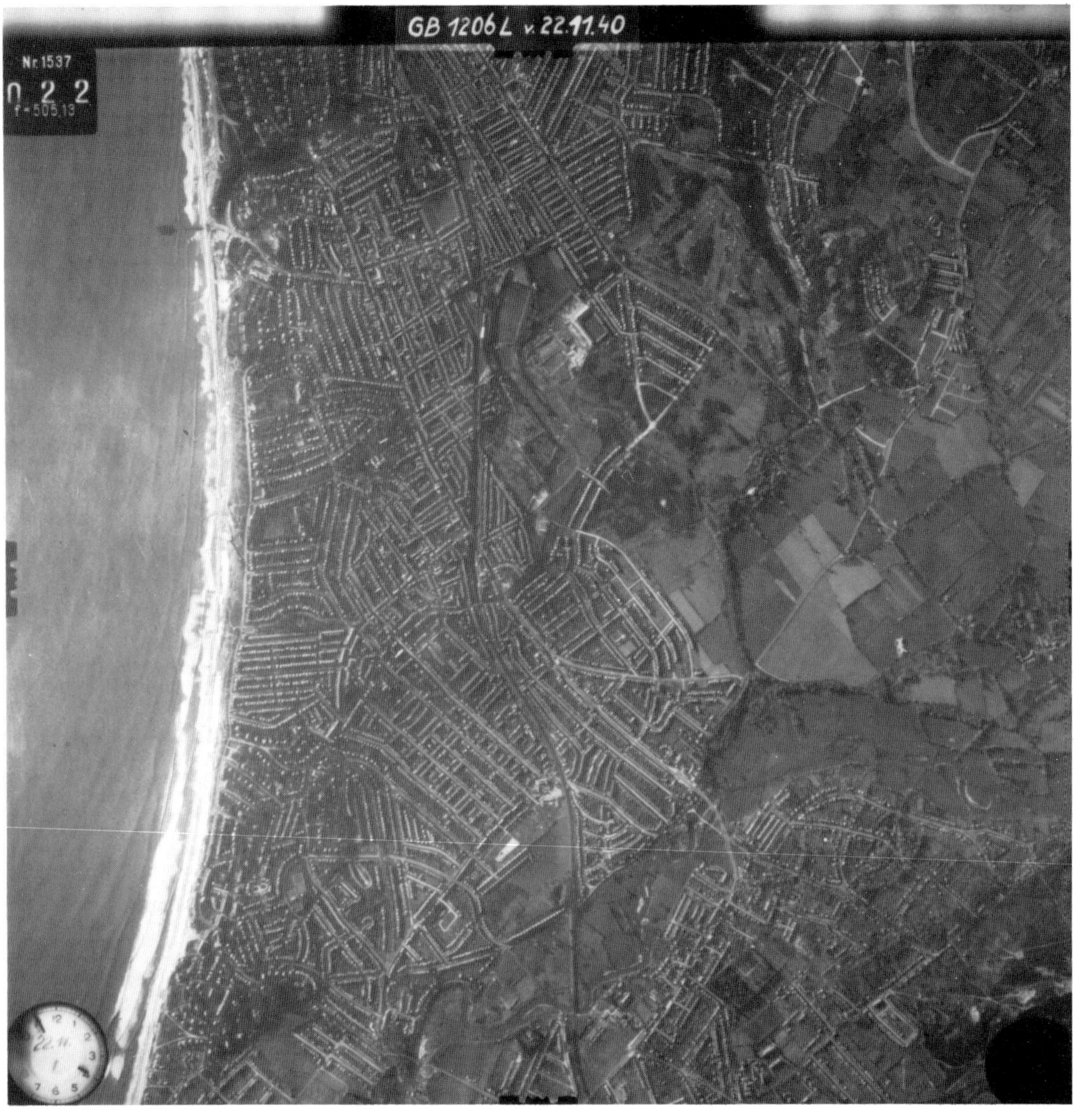

Bournemouth
22nd November 1940
Bournemouth and Boscombe
GX 1049 222

DORSET

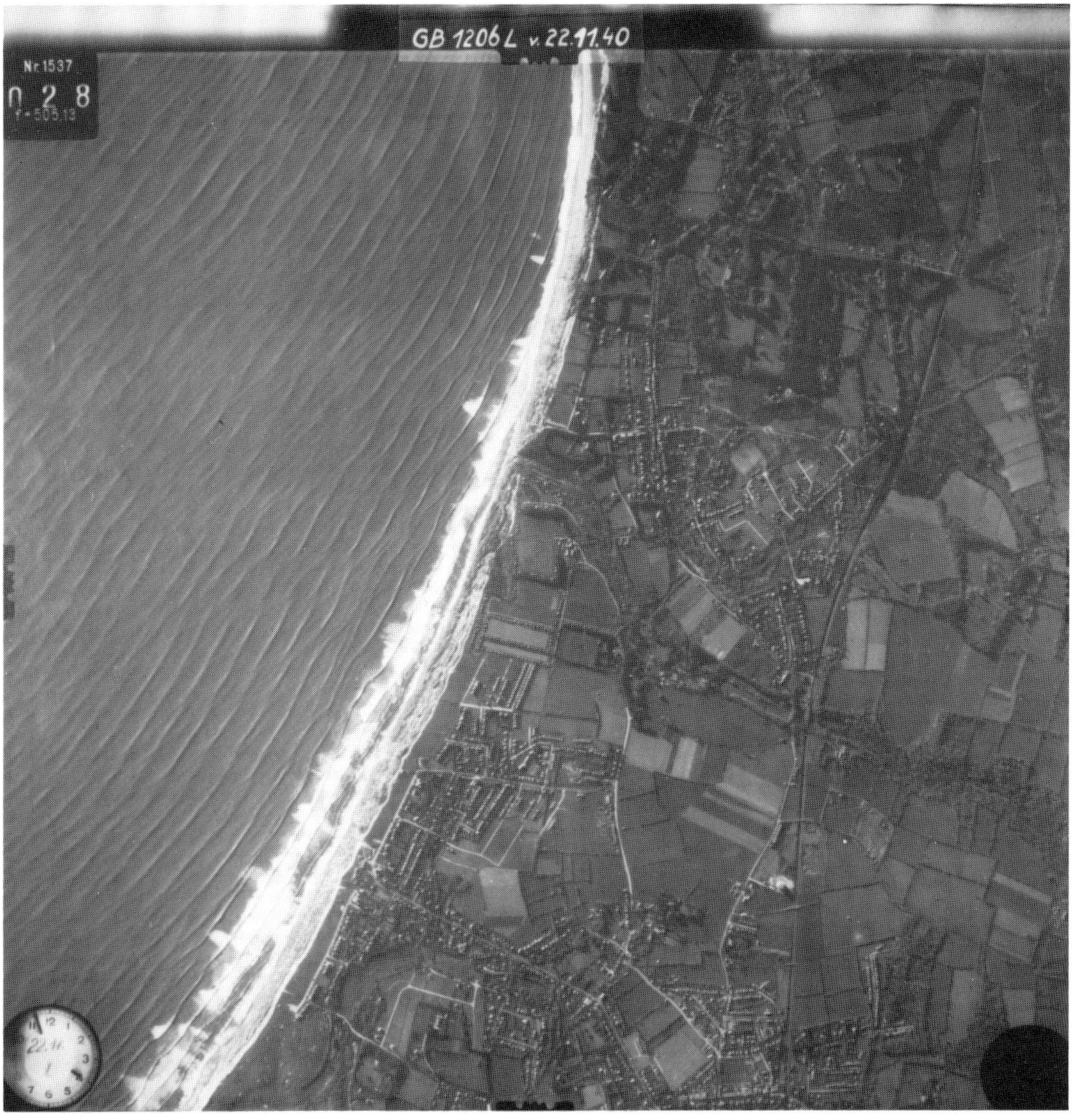

Bournemouth
22nd November 1940
Highcliffe, Chewton Bunny and Barton-on-Sea
GX 1049 028

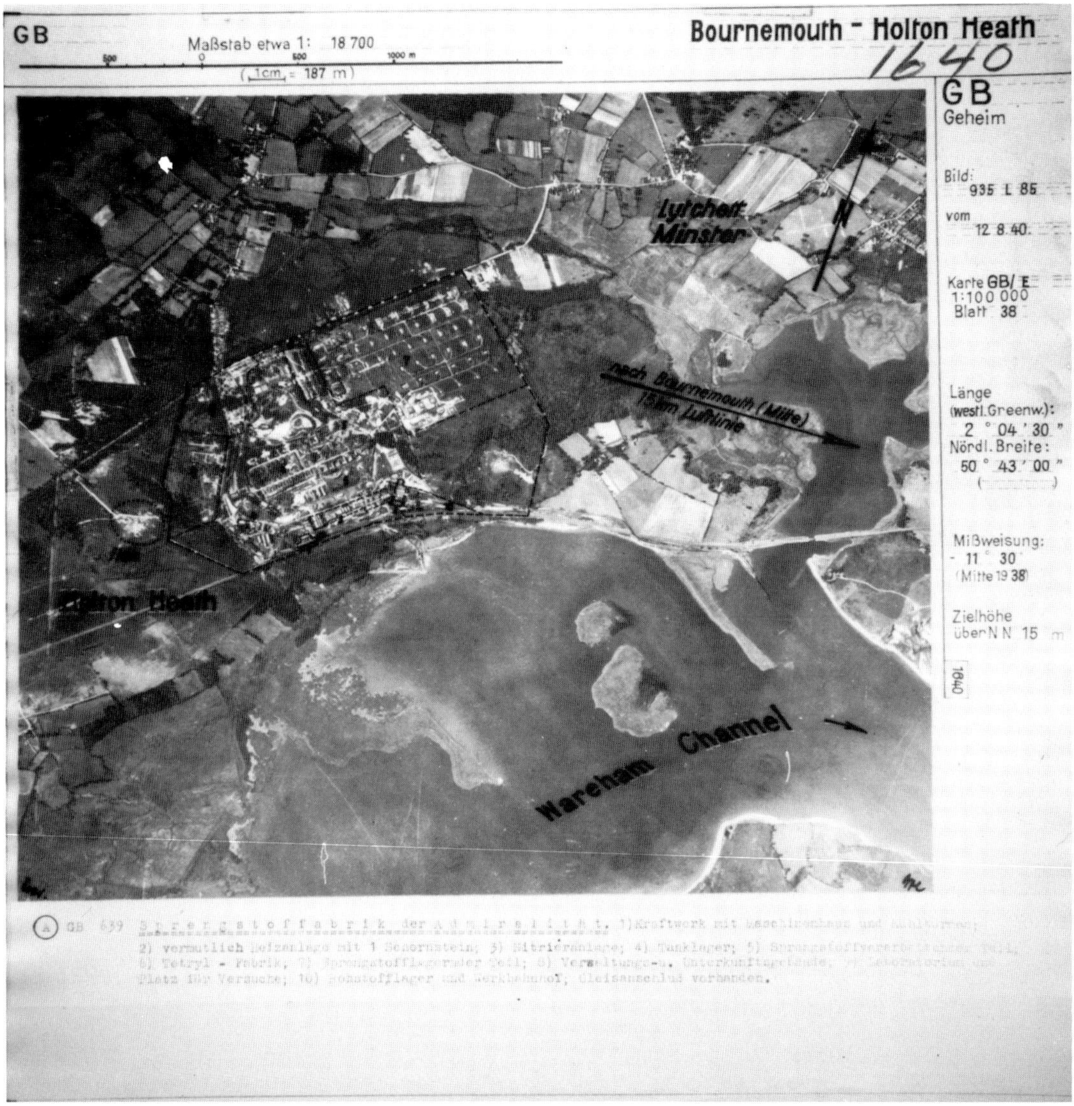

Bournemouth
12th August 1940
Holton Heath
Admiralty cordite and explosives works
TN 1640
Comment

The Naval Cordite works were constructed at Holton Heath in 1915, some of the original chemical plant was of German manufacture. The company built two decoy factories some distance from the original plant to divert the bombers. During one raid waste cordite was set ablaze at the decoy site and the Luftwaffe added a further 200 bombs to the dummy target.

GB 45157 b c | **Bridport** | Karte 1 : 100 000
N. f. D. | Hafenanlage | Engl. Bl. 37 c

Bild Nr. F812b/40/265v **Geogr. Lage:** 2° 46' W, 50° 42' N, **Höhe ü. d. M.** – m Stand: I. 41.

250 0 250 500 m

Maßstab etwa 1 : 6500 (1 cm = 65 m) Lfl. Kdo. 3

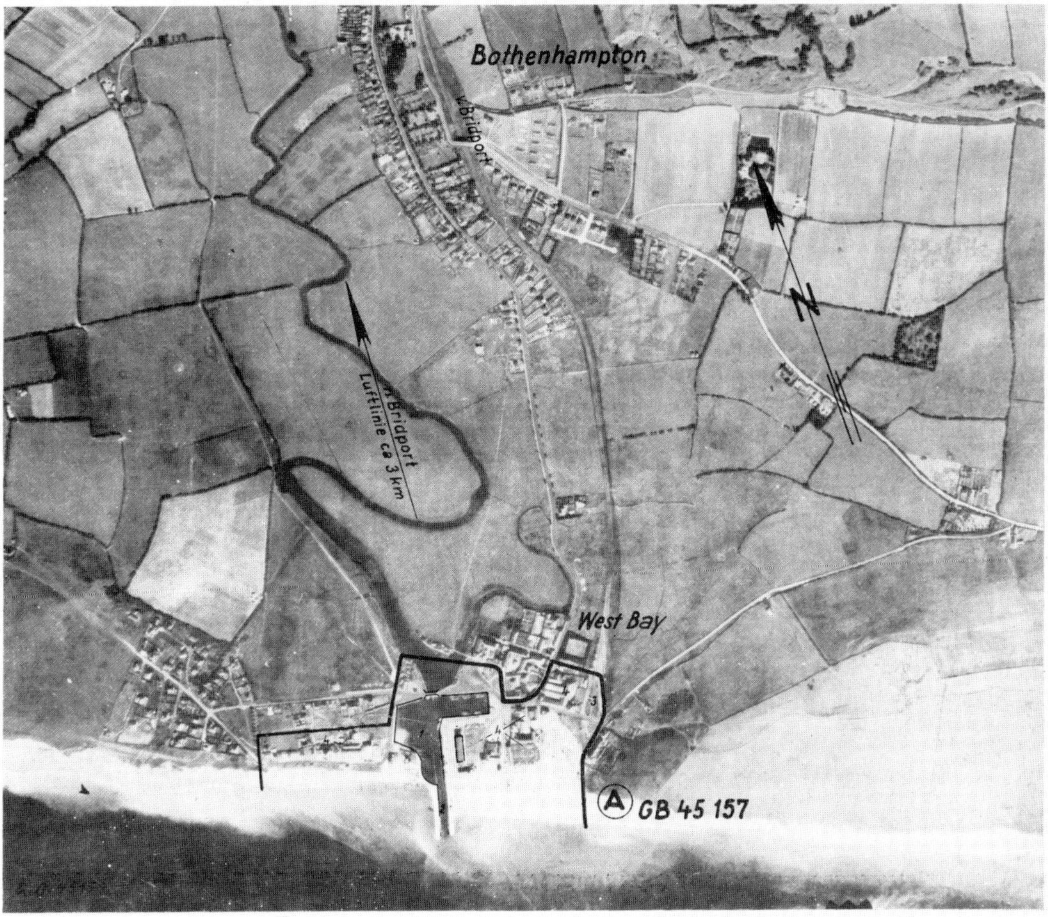

(A) GB 45 157 Hafenanlage

1) Hafenbecken
2) Hafeneinfahrt etwa 15 m breit
3) Bahnhofsanlage
4) Lagergebäude etwa 4 700 qm

Bridport
1940
West Bay Harbour and Bothenhampton
GB 45157

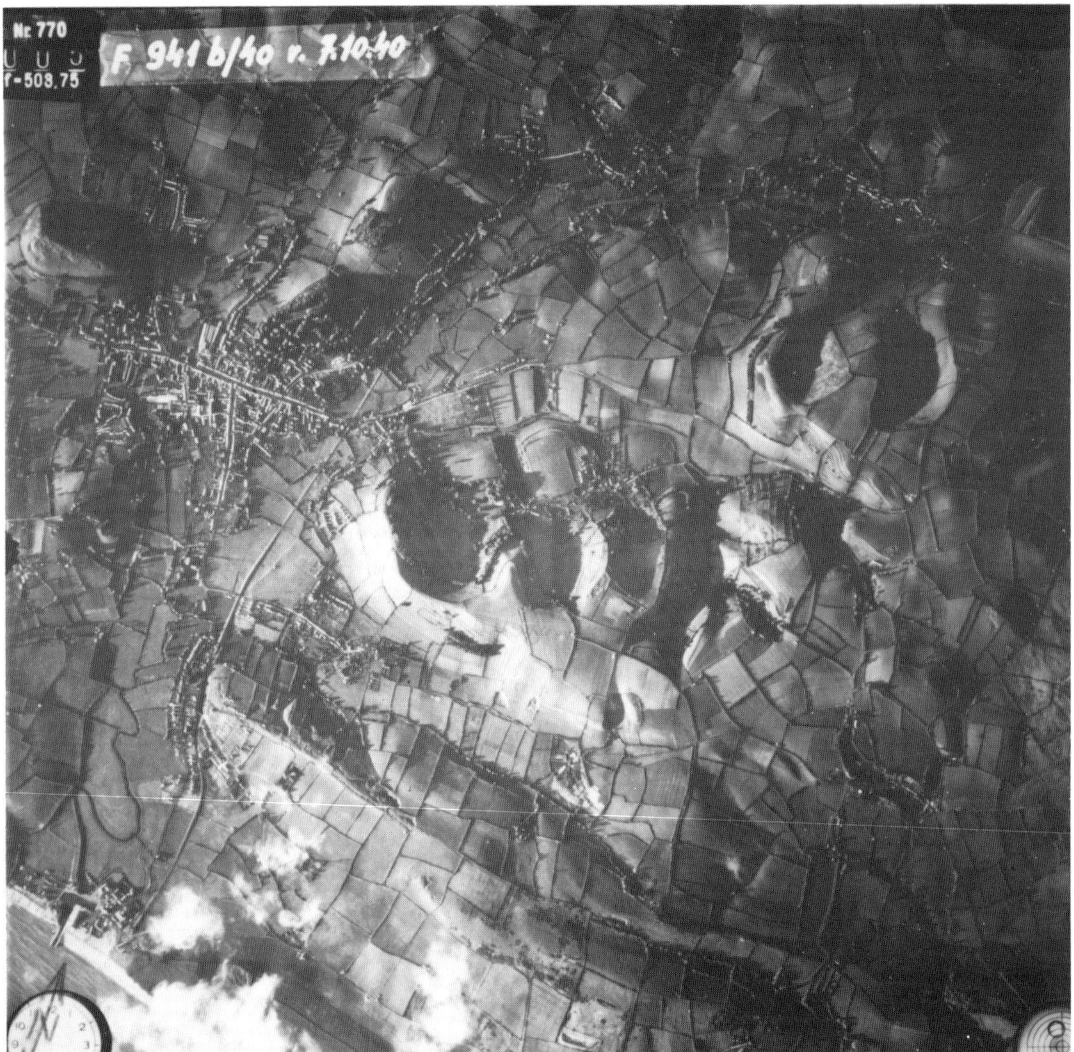

Bridport
7th October 1940
Bridport, West Bay and Bothenhampton
GX 10288 005

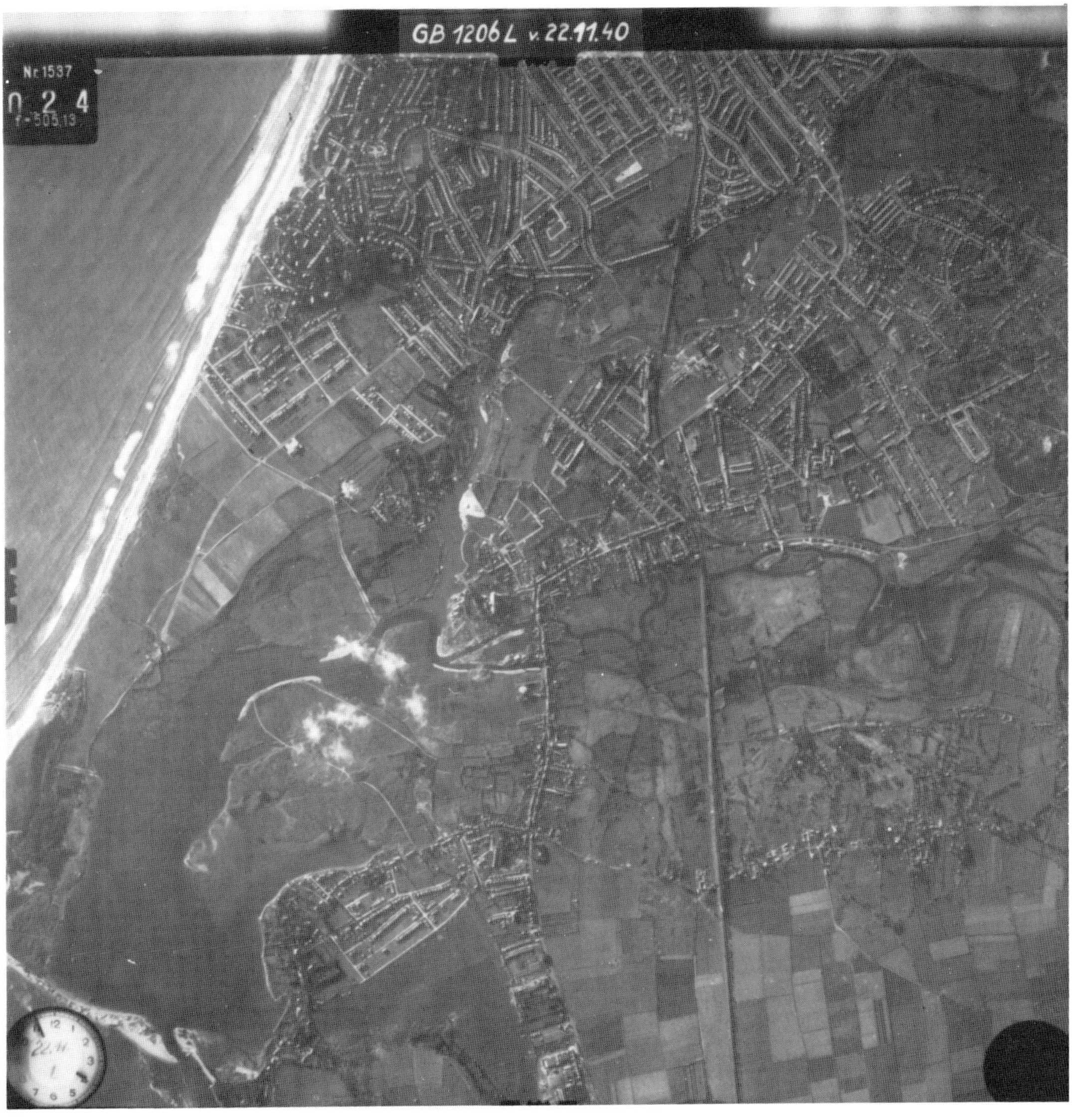

Christchurch
22nd November 1940
Christchurch, Hengistbury Head and Mudeford
GX 10492 024

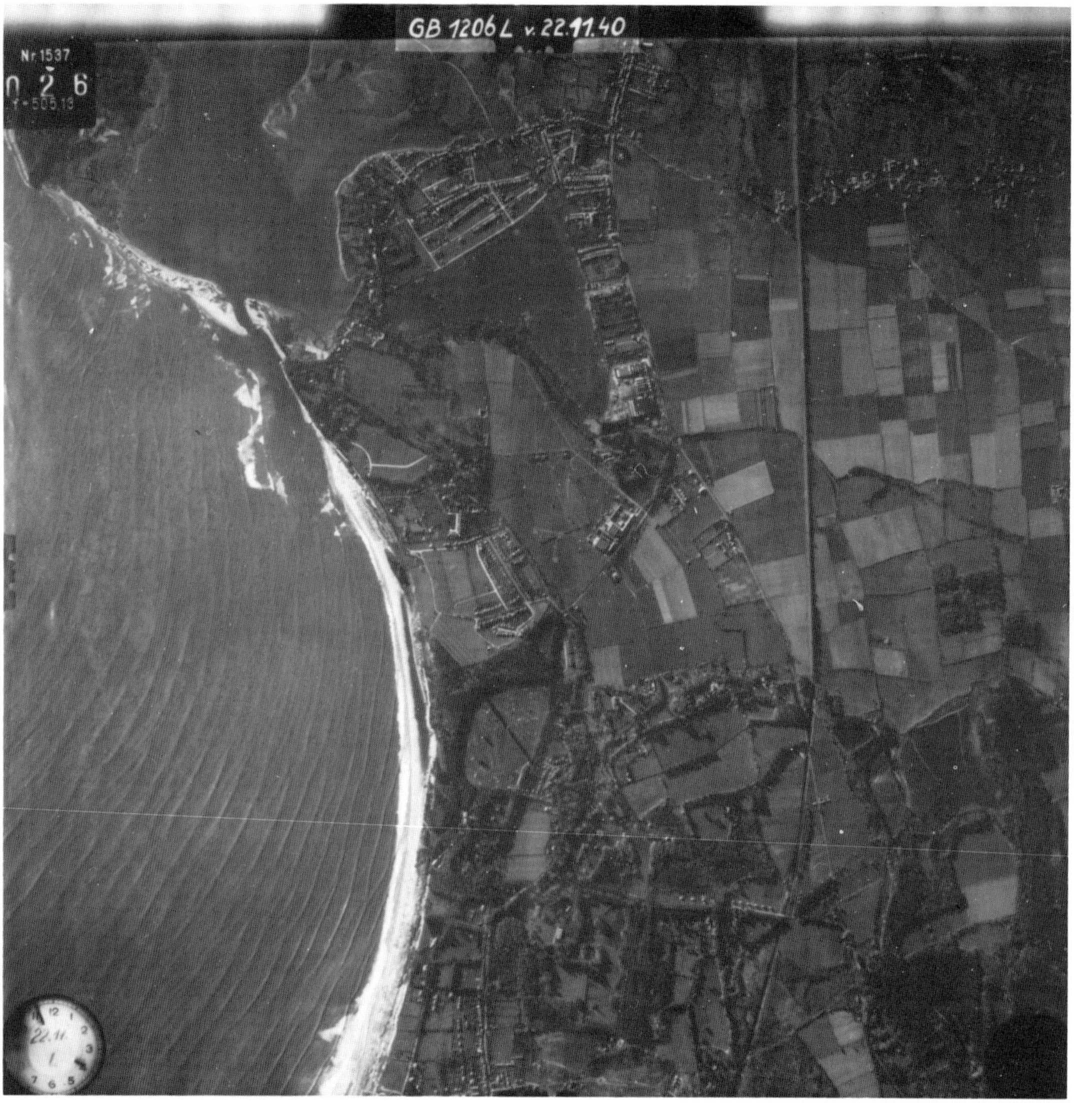

Christchurch
22nd November 1940
Christchurch, Mudeford and Highcliffe
GX 10492 026

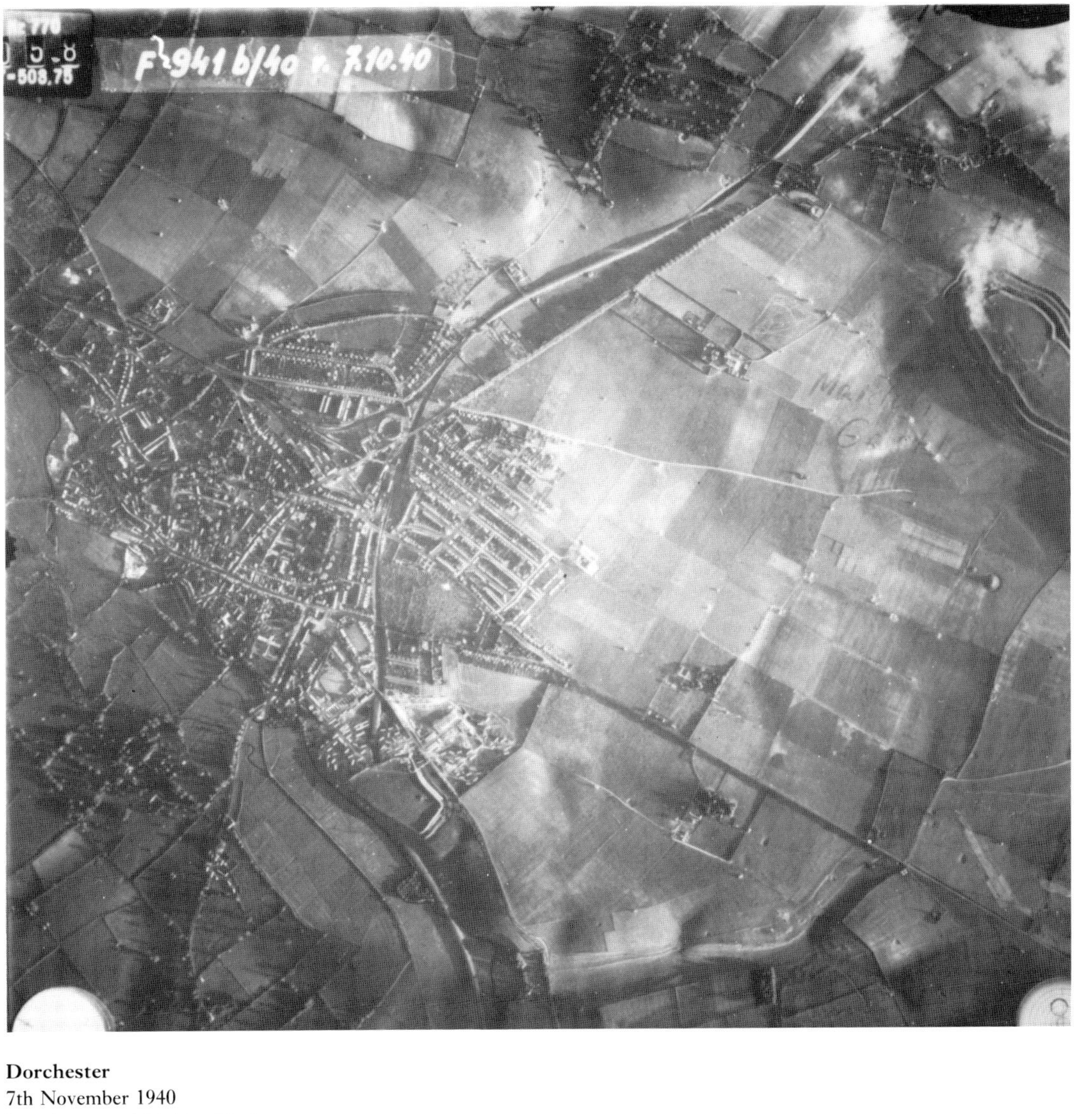

Dorchester
7th November 1940
Dorchester and Maiden Castle
GX 10288 058

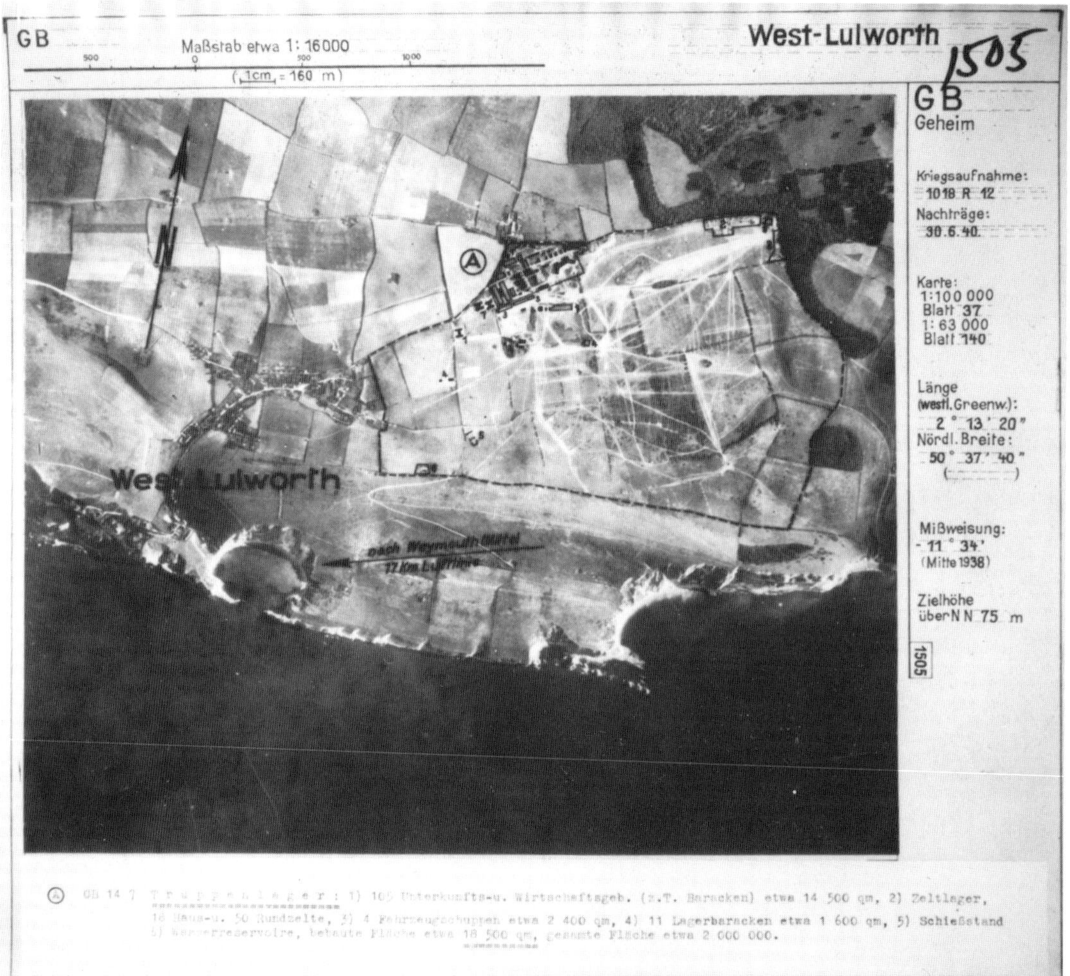

Lulworth Cove
3rd September 1940
Lulworth Cove, army firing ranges and barracks.

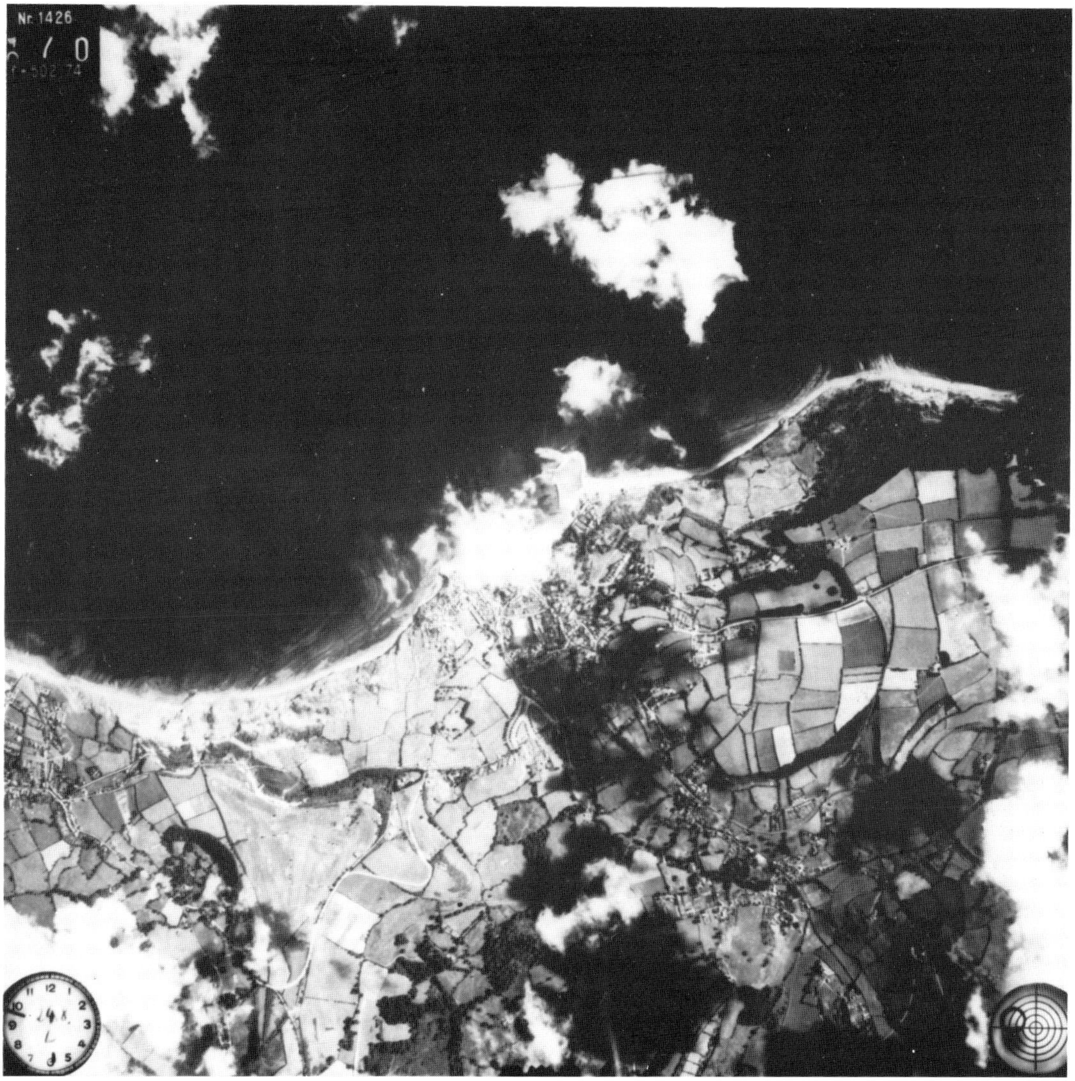

Lyme Regis
24th August 1940
Town and cliffs to the east
GX 10105 70
Comment
This area of Dorset has always suffered from land slip and erosion. The cliffs between Lyme Regis and Charmouth contain the largest mud-flows in Europe. This aerial photograph taken over fifty years ago shows features such as the coastal road between Charmouth and Lyme Regis which slid into the sea in 1952. The fields on the eastern edge of the town are now developed and built on.

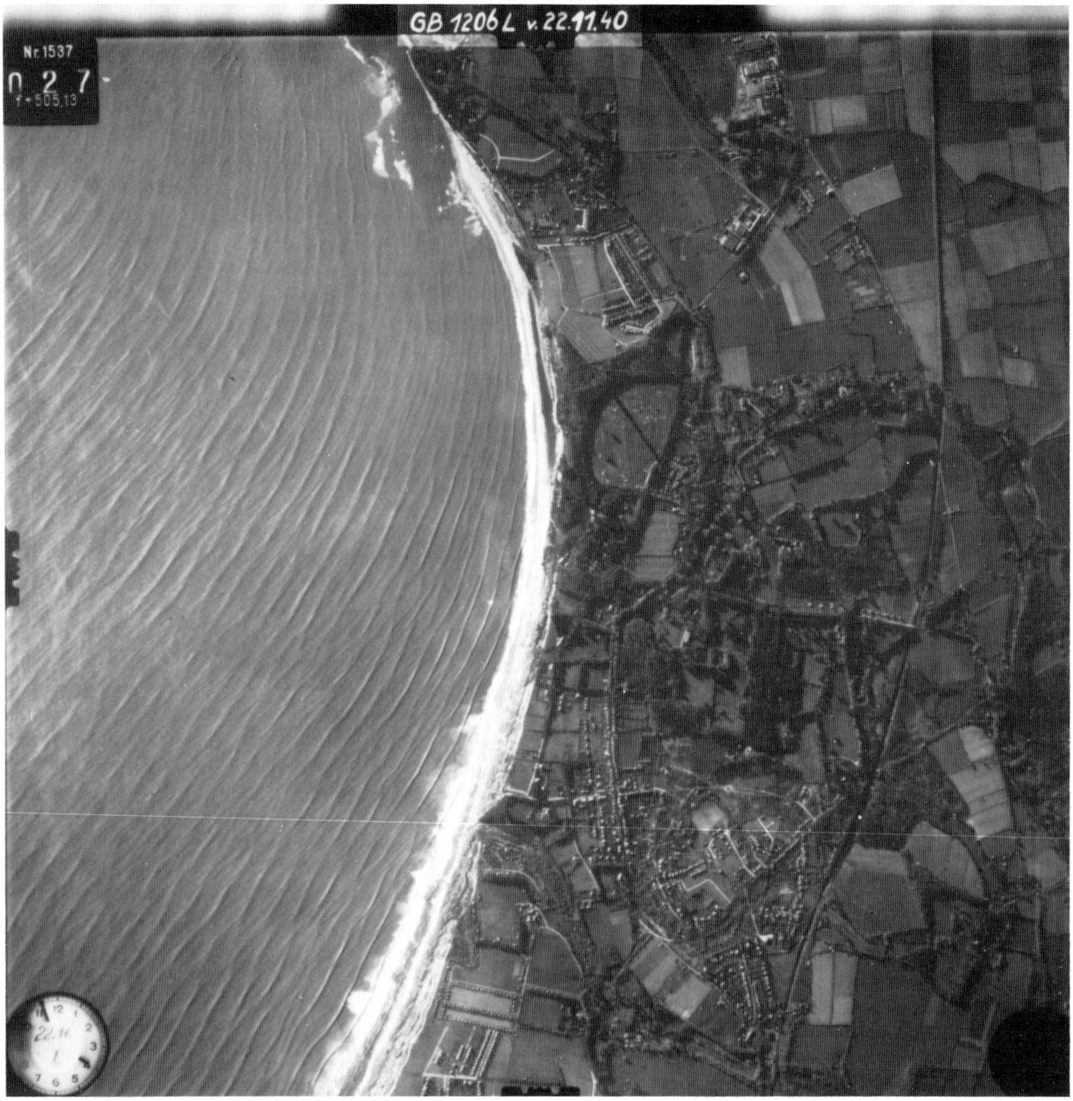

Highcliffe-Mudeford
22nd November 1940

GX 10492 027

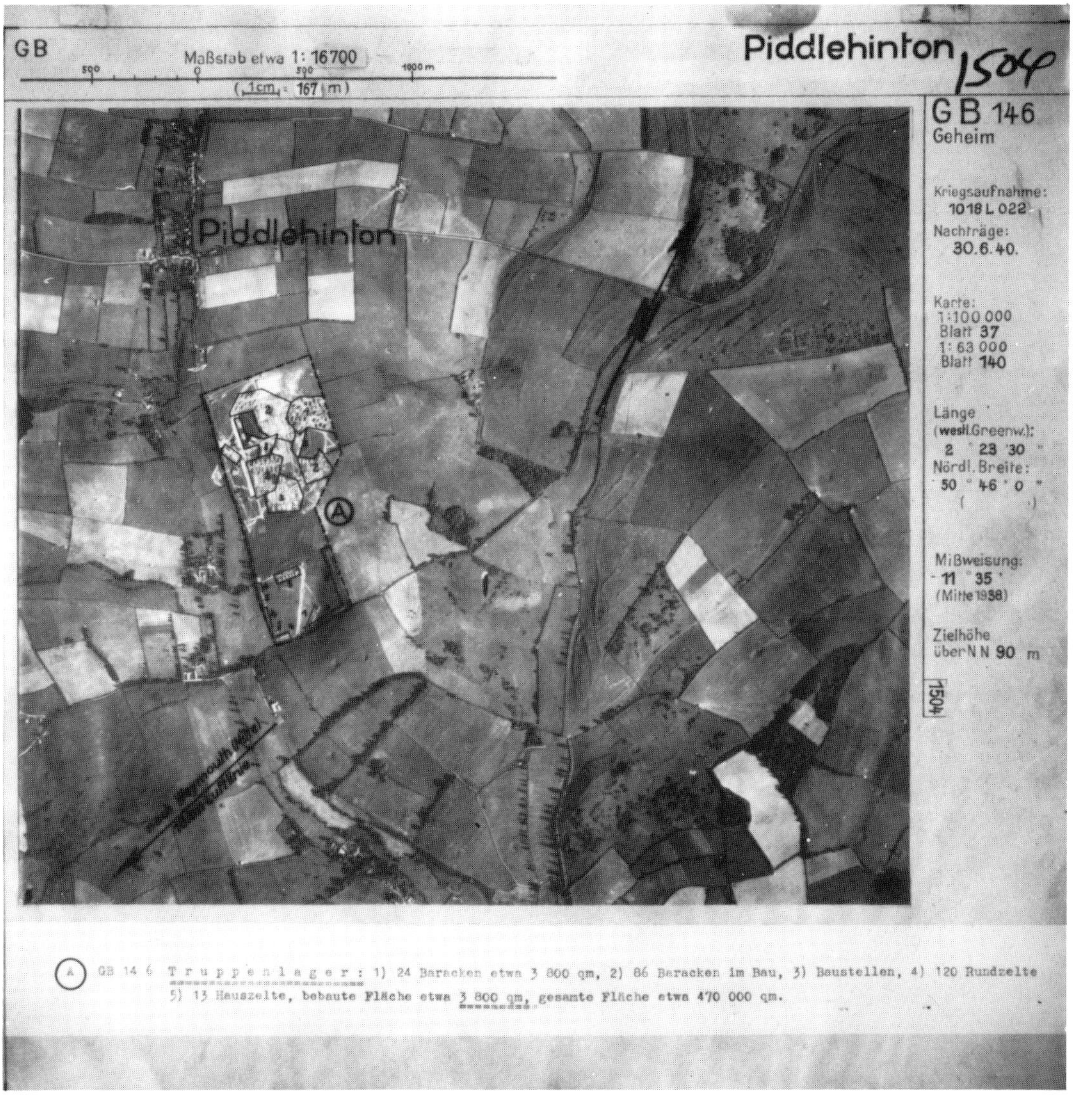

Piddlehinton
30th June 1940
Troop depot
TN 1504

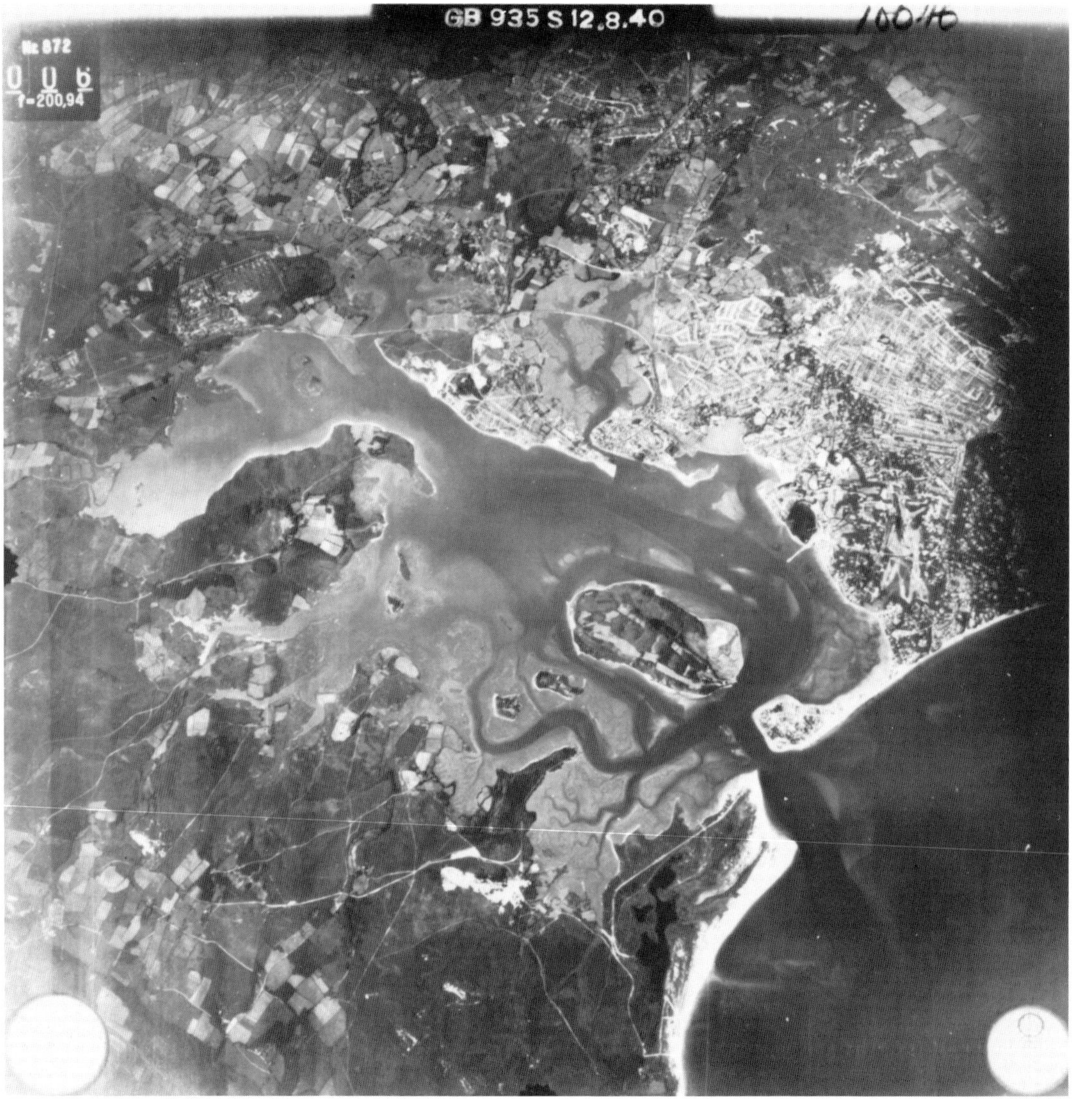

Poole
12th August 1940
Poole Harbour
GX 10046 6

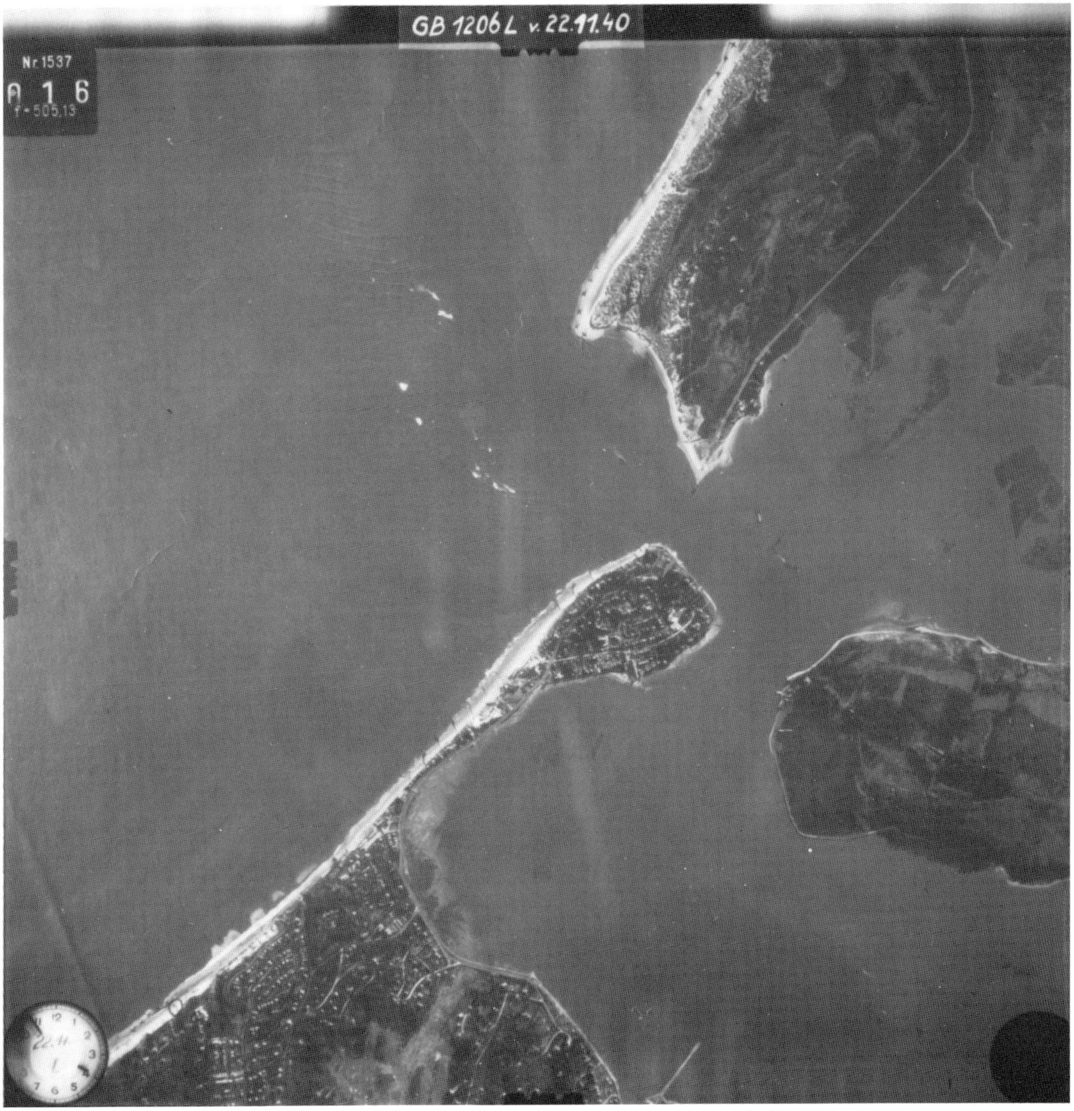

Poole
22nd November 1940
Sandbanks, Studland and Brownsea Island
GX 104920 16
Comment
Poole became one of the most important military centres during the second World War. Its wide and expansive harbour was both ideal for the invasion of Britain and as safe anchorage for the forces that led to liberation of France. The Luftwaffe took numerous aerial photographs of the harbour which was already used by Imperial Airways for the flying-boat service to the far corners of the empire. Throughout the war the area was regularly bombed. A decoy Poole was built on Brownsea Island to entice the Luftwaffe away which proved highly successful. If you look at the Island you can see the star shaped craters of the bombs. In recent years both Poole and Bournemouth have expanded and the suburbs have spread further into the rural hinterland. Oil has been discovered by B.P. If only the allies had known in 1944 that below their barges, tanks and ships lay a vast lake of underground oil.

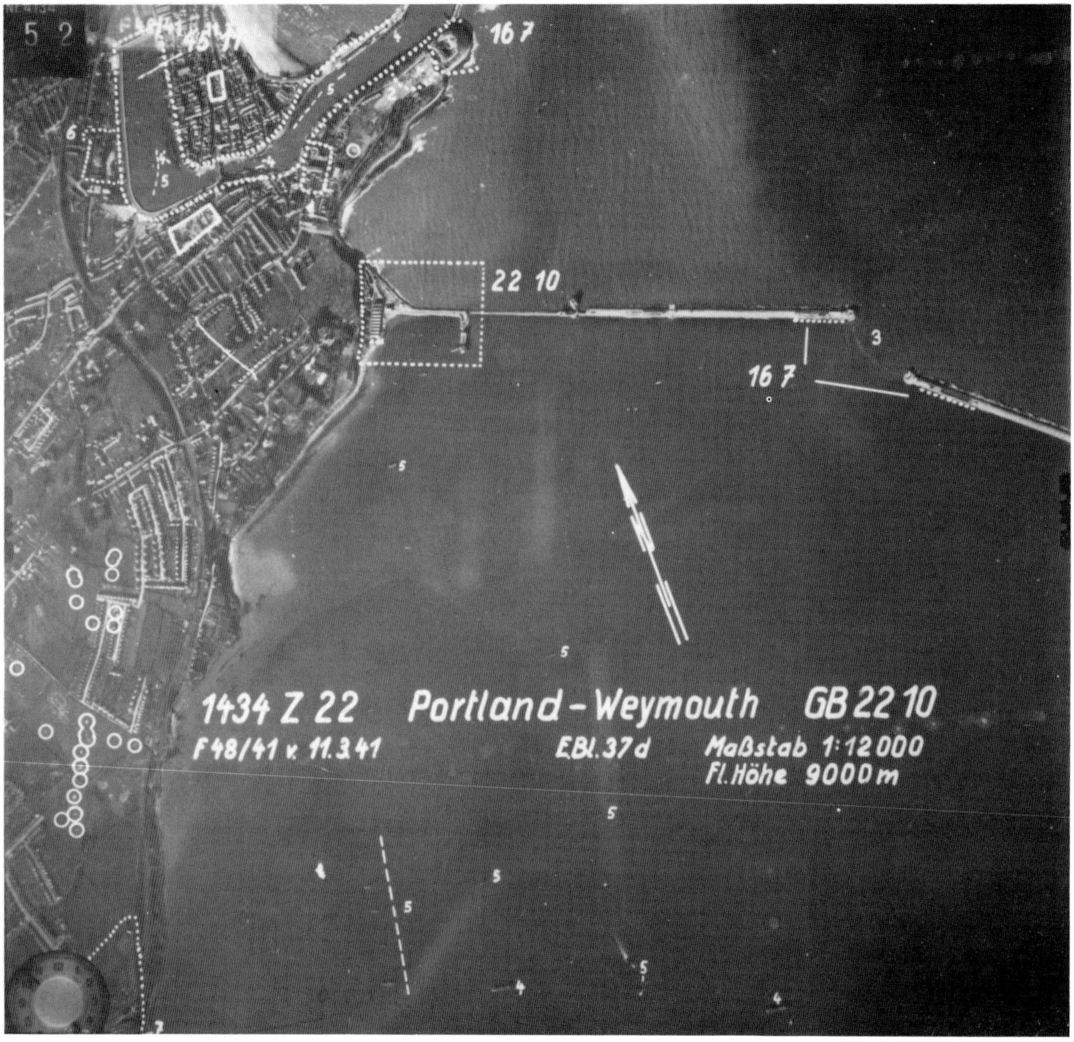

Portland
11th March 1941
Weymouth, Rodwell and Portland Breakwater
GX 11921 052

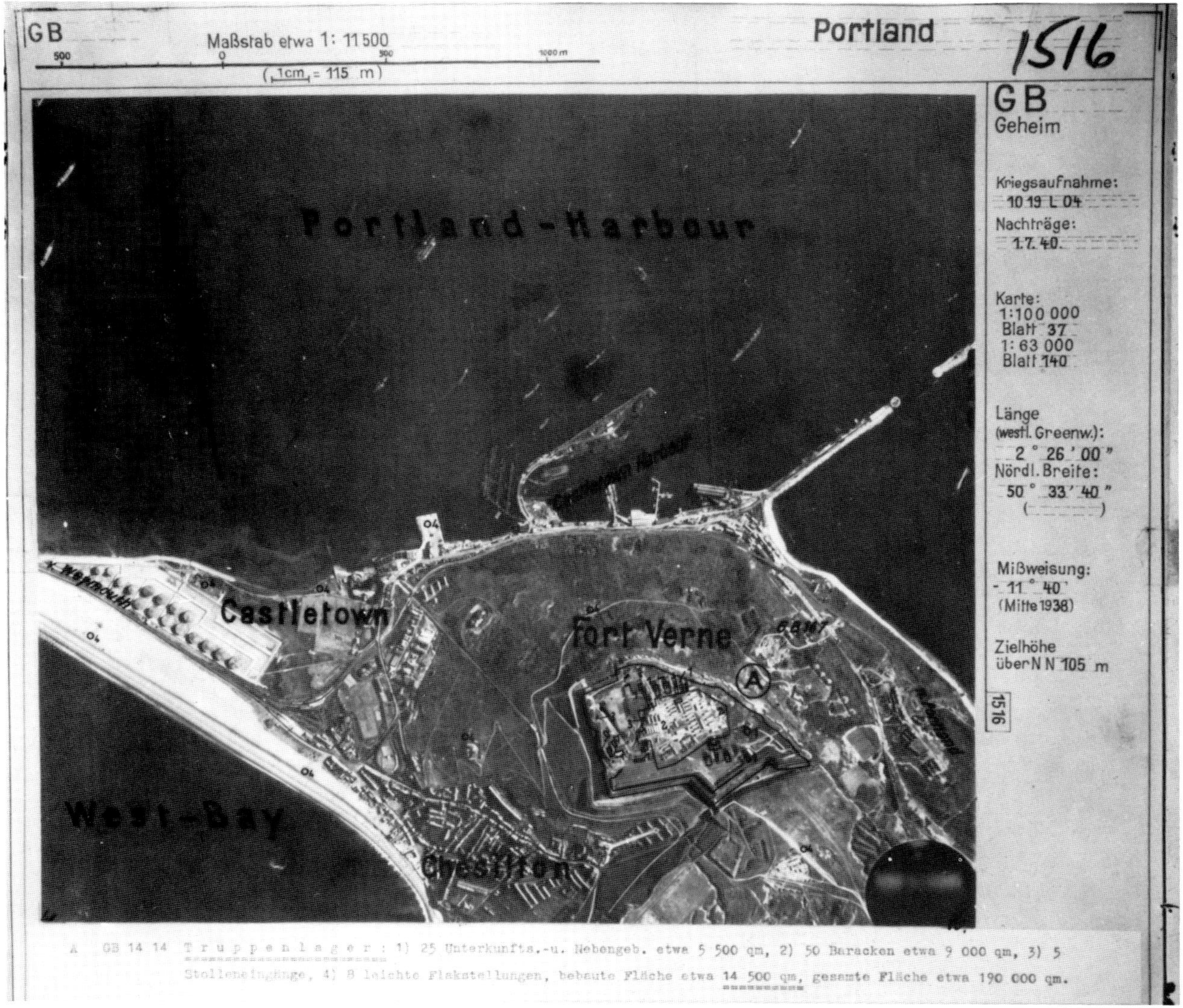

Portland

1st July 1940

Portland Naval Base, Castletown, Fortuneswell and The Verne Prison.

TN 1516

Comment

The Verne was constructed in 1861. The prominent hill overlooking Portland harbour attracted many settlers from the early British tribes to the Romans. While digging for the foundations of The Verne Citadel many artefacts were found from the early inhabitants of this impressive hill. The Verne covers 56 acres and the building consumed 3 million convict hand made bricks. The photograph shows the numerous scars of the local stone extraction industry. The first recorded attack on Portland was on the 30th June 1940, when a force of twenty Stuka dive bombers attacked the naval base.

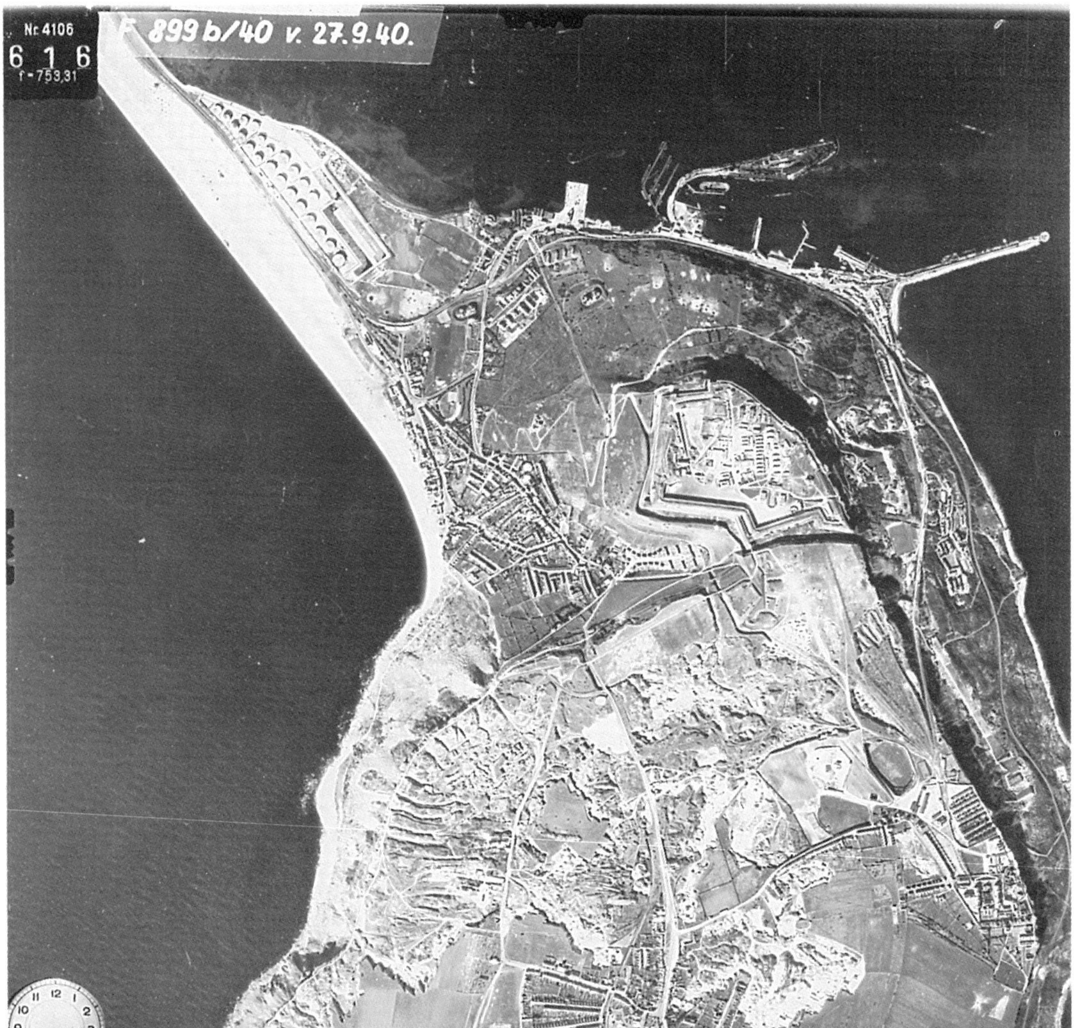

Portland
27th September 1940
Fortuneswell and The Verne Prison
GX 110332 616
Comment
Hermann Goering's nephew, Oberleutnant H-D Goering was shot down in a Messerschmitt Bf110C at The Verne, Portland, at 12.00 hours on July 11th, 1940. The aircraft plunged to the ground with such force that no trace was found of Oberleutnant Goering or his gunner Unteroffixer Zimmerman.

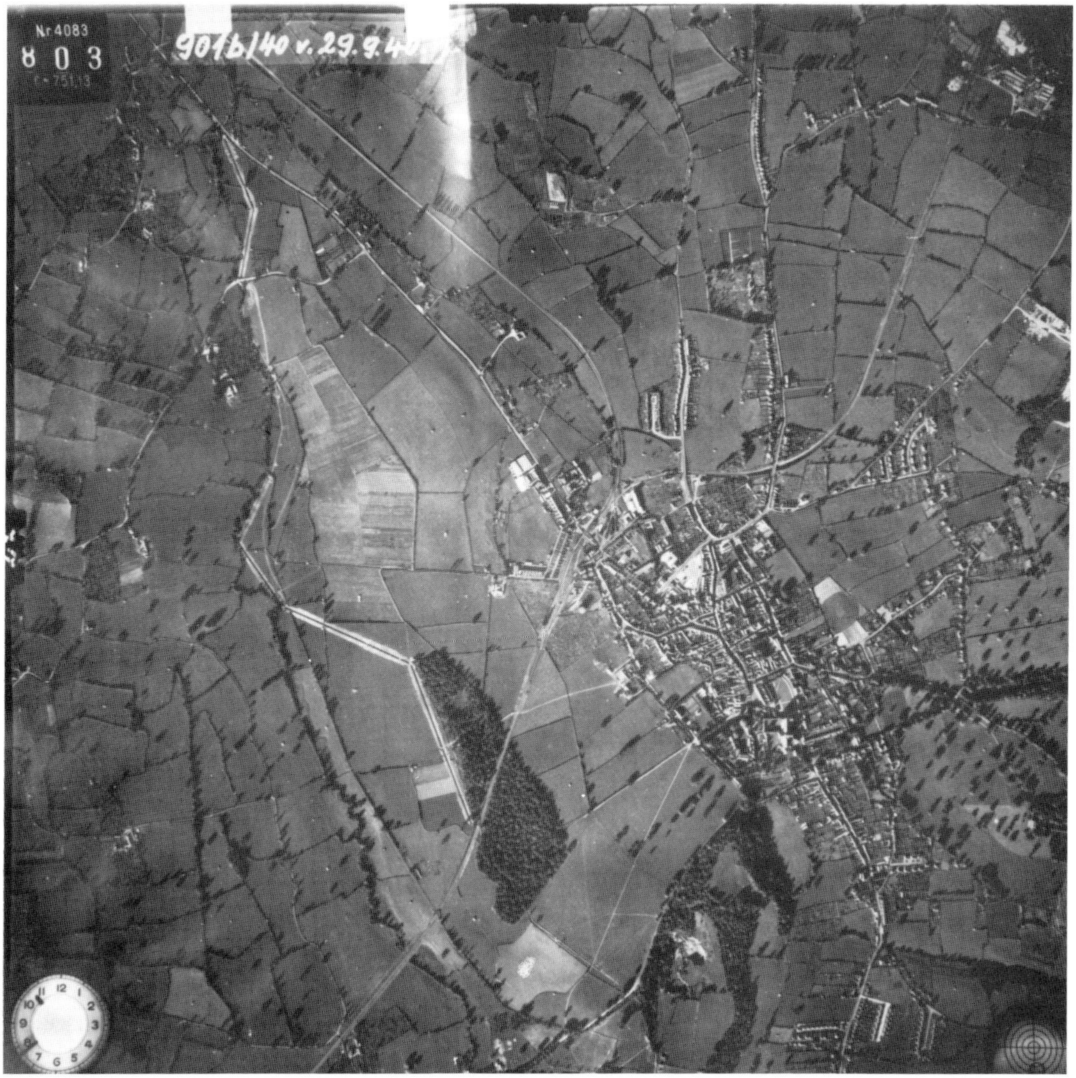

Sherborne
29th September 1940
Sherborne town
GX 10313 803

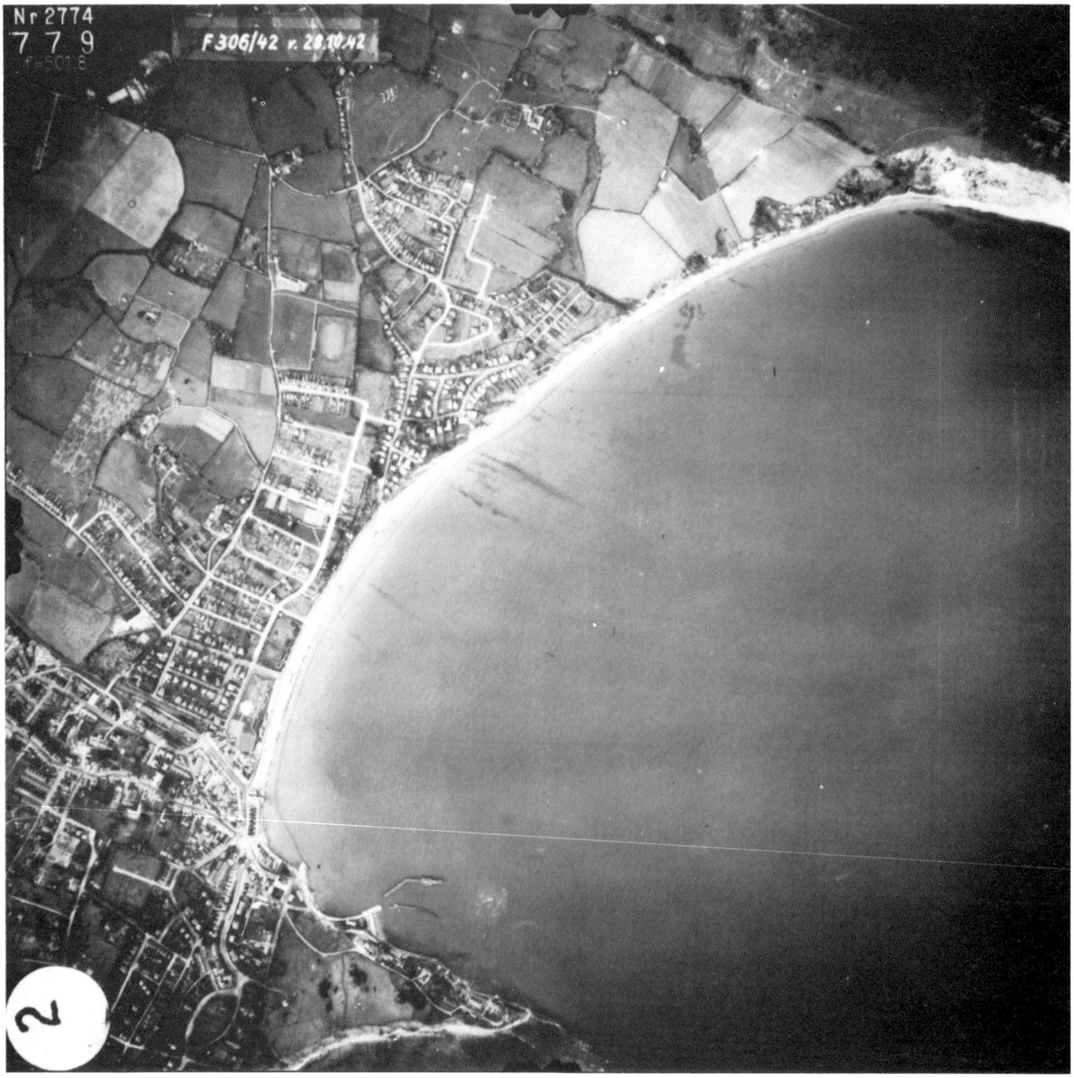

Swanage
28th November 1942
Sea front and town centre
GX 12065 779
Comment
At the bottom of the picture is Peveril Point. At the end of the Point are the old coast guard cottages and the old slipway for the lifeboat. You can see from the photograph that the pier has been cut in the middle to hinder any German beach landings. Along the beach can be seen the snaking black outline of the obstacles. Originally Swanage grew as a small fishing and quarrying village. In the nineteenth century Swanage attracted holiday makers which led to the boom in guest houses. After the war a further building boom covered many of the fields visible in this photograph in houses.

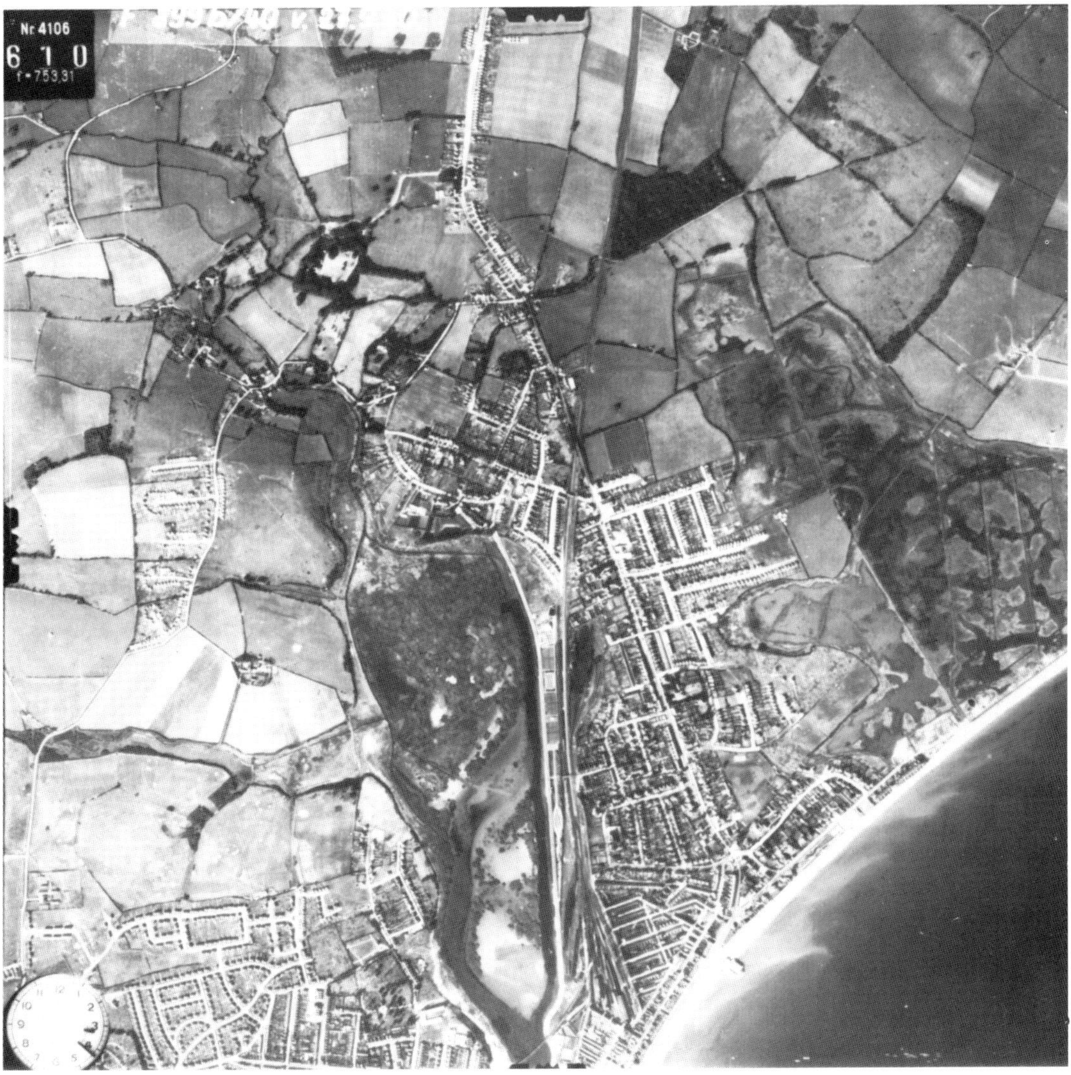

Weymouth
27th September 1940
Weymouth Harbour,
Melcombe Regis and Lodmoor
GX 110332 610
Comment
The start of the Battle of Britain was on the 8th of August, when the Luftwaffe launched an initial offensive that lasted till the 12th of August with a series of massive attacks on a 500 mile arc from Weymouth to Newcastle.

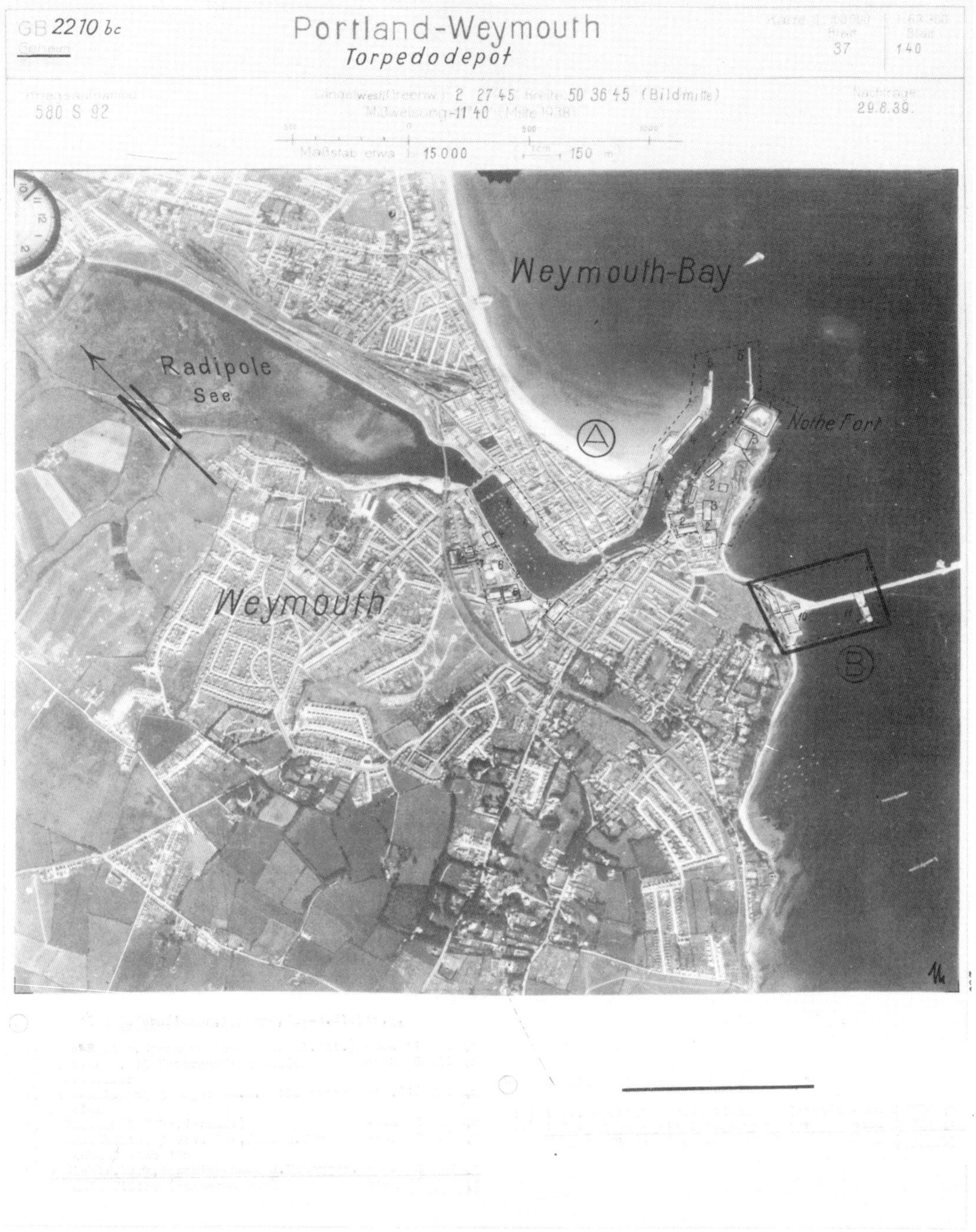

Weymouth
29th August 1939
Harbour and electricity works
TN 200
Comment
Weymouth in 1940 was still a small coastal town. The harbour looks deserted and the old Portland railway bridge is still in use, of which now only the stumps remain. During the eleven months of the operation leading up to and after the D-Day landings Weymouth and Portland harbours handled over 500,000 troops, 145,000 vehicles and vast quantities of supplies.

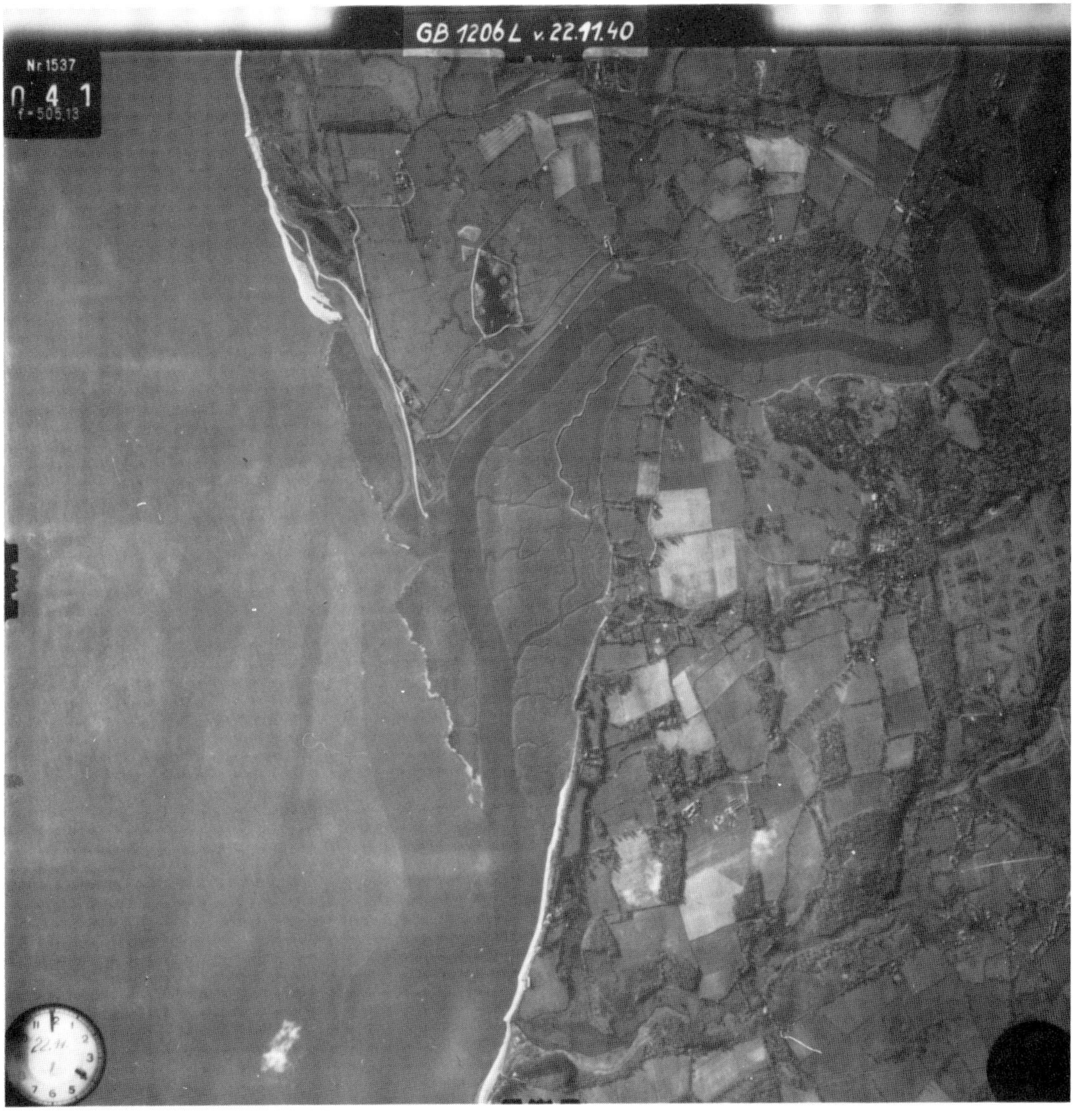

Beaulieu Estuary
22nd November 1940
The Beaulieu Estuary and small village of Exbury
GX 10492 041

HAMPSHIRE

GB 2135 b c Geheim	**Portsmouth** *Unterird. Tanklager*	Karte 1 : 100 000 Engl. Bl. 38 b

Bild Nr. 516 Z 21 **Geogr. Lage** 1° 6' W, 50° 51' N, **Höhe ü. d. M.** 91 m **Stand** VIII. 40.

Maßstab etwa 1 : 16 000 (1 cm = 160 m)

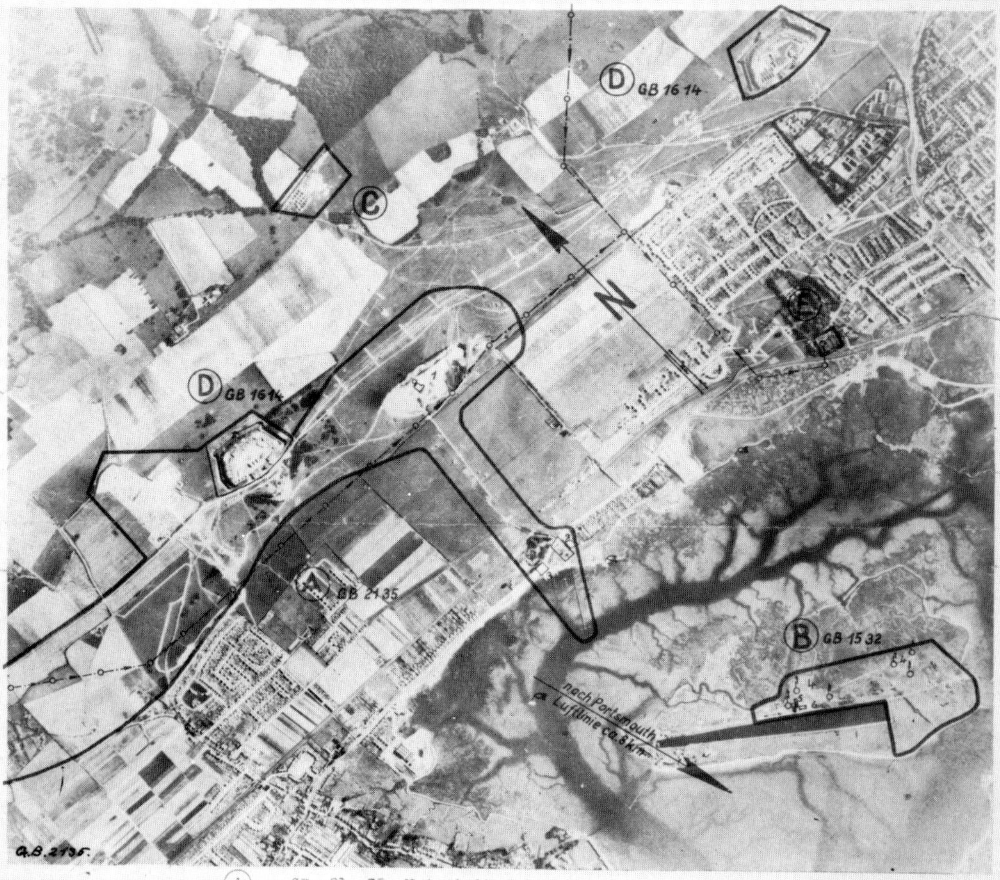

(A) GB 21 35 Unterirdisches Tanklager
1) Pumpstation und Schornstein
2) Tanklager Paulsgrove Quay (3 kleine Tanks)
3) Ölpumpstation

(B) GB 15 32 Portchester (Portsmouth) Großfunkstelle
4) 6 Sendemaste
5) Sendehaus
6) Verwaltungsgebäude
Gesamtfläche etwa 159 000 qm

(C) schwere Flakstellung

(D) GB 16 14 2 Befestigungsanlagen der Portsdown - Linie

(E) Elektrische Umschaltanlage und Fernleitung

1940 GERMAN TARGET PHOTO OF PORTSMOUTH

Portsmouth

Porchester Castle, Torpedo test tank and wireless station
GB 2135

GB 12 32 b c
N. f. D.

Portsmouth

5 Trockendocks im Bassin 3

Karte 1:100 000
Engl. Bl. 38b

Bild Nr. 325 Z 45 Geogr. Lage 1° 06' W, 50° 48' N, Höhe ü. d. M. — m Stand VIII. 40

Maßstab etwa 1: 15 500 (1 cm = 155 m)

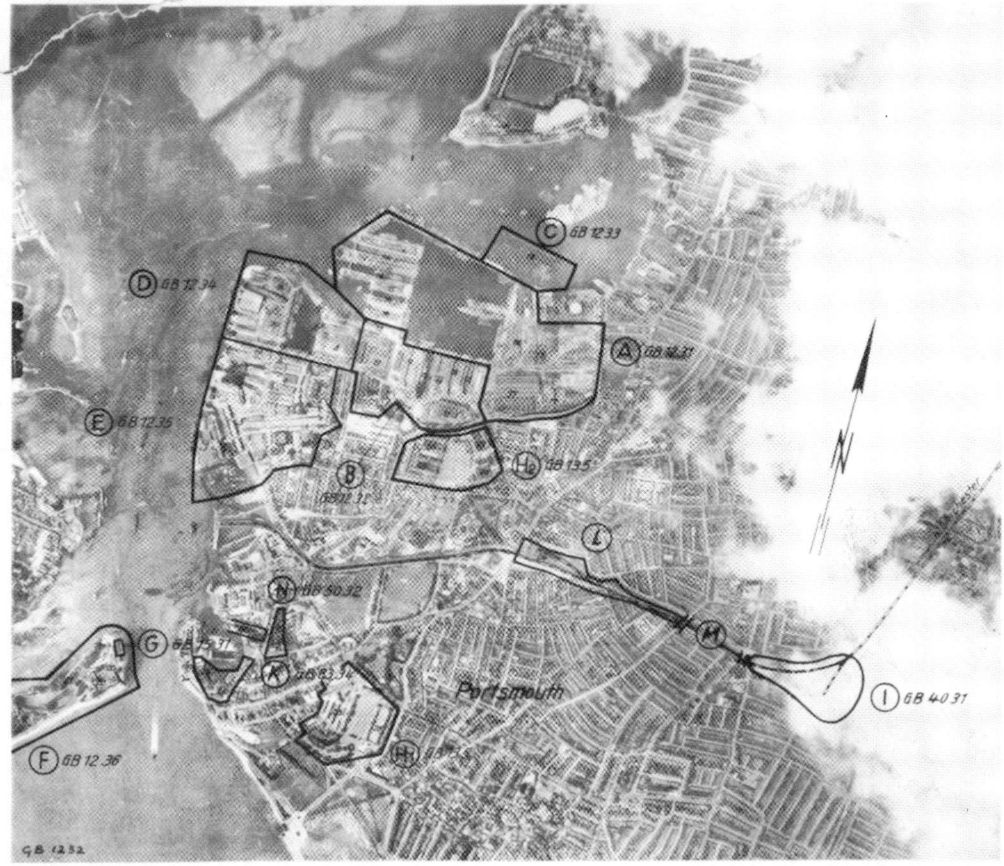

(A)	GB	12 31	4 Dockschleusen mit Werkstätten 14) 4 Schleusen 15) Kraftquelle d. Werkstätten 16) Ausrüstungsmagazin 17) Werkstatthallen
(B)	GB	12 32	5 Trockendocks im Bassin 3 12) 5 Docks 13) Werkstatthallen
(C)	GB	12 33	Schwimmdock der Staatswerft 18) Schwimmdock
(D)	GB	12 34	Bassin 2 der Staatswerft 6) Grösserer Bauhelling 7) 4 Kleine Bauhellinge, davon 2 überdacht 8) 2 Ausrüstungsmagazine 9) 4 Trockendocks 10) Kraftquelle 11) Eingangstor z. Bassin
(E)	GB	12 35	Bassin 1 der Staatswerft 1) Einfahrt z. Bassin
(F)	GB	12 36	U-Boothafen am Haslar Lake 19) Stützpunkte für Räumboote 20) U-Bootschule u. Sitz des Admirals d. U-Boote 21) Schwimmdock
(G)	GB	15 31	Grossfunkstelle
(H1) (H2)	GB	13 5	Artilleriekaserne u. Kaserne 28) Unterkunfts-u. Stallgebäude
(I)	GB	40 31	Bahn-u. Güterstation Fratton
(K)	GB	83 34	Werft von Vosper, P.-Gosport 25) Hauptanlage m. Slips u. Bauhellingen 26) Grosse Werkstatthalle 27) Teilanlage m. Trockendock u. kleinen Werkstätten
(L)	GB		Personenbahnhof 24) Bahnhofshalle
(M)	GB		2 Strassenüberführungen

Portsmouth

Portsmouth Naval Base and docks
GB 1232

GB 13 8 b c
Nur für den Dienstgebrauch
Bild Nr. 1426 Z 10
Aufnahme vom 3. 3. 41

Portsmouth-Hilsea

Kasernen

Länge (westl. Greenw.): 1° 04′ Nördl. Breite: 50° 49′ 30″
Zielhöhe über NN 3 m

Lfl. Kdo. 3 September 1941
Karte 1:100000.
GB/E Bl. 38 b

500 0 500 1000 m
Maßstab 1: 17500

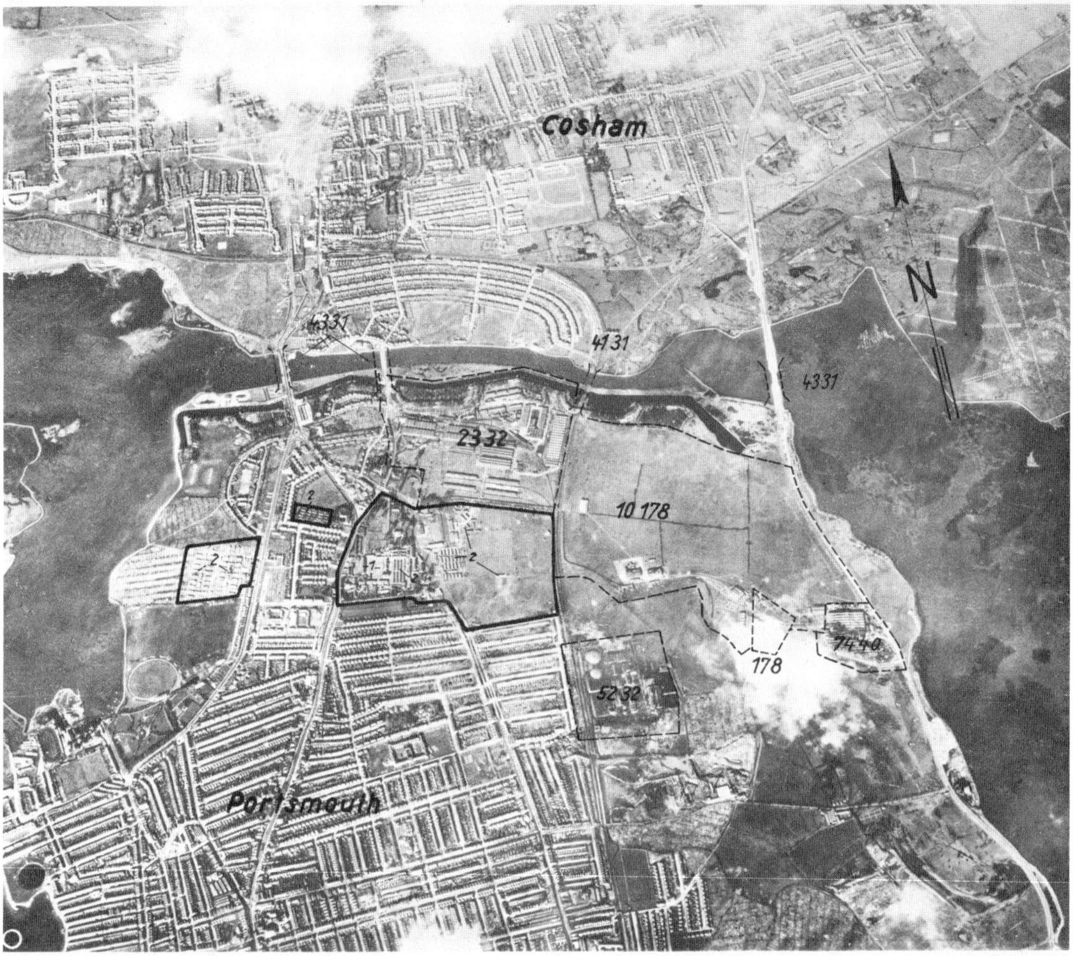

GB 138	Kasernen		
	1. 6 Kasernengebäude, massiv	etwa	4 000 qm
	2. 100 Baracken	etwa	20 700 qm
	Bebaute Fläche	etwa	24 700 qm
	Gesamtfläche	etwa	525 000 qm

GB 10 178	Flugplatz Portsmouth
GB 17 8	Peilanlage
GB 41 31	Eisenbahnbrücke
GB 43 31	2 Straßenbrücken, 1 Straßendamm
GB 52 32	Gaswerk Hilsea
GB 74 40	Flugzeugzellenwerk Portsmouth-Hilsea

Portsmouth
3rd September 1941
Portsmouth, Hilsea and Cosham
GB 138

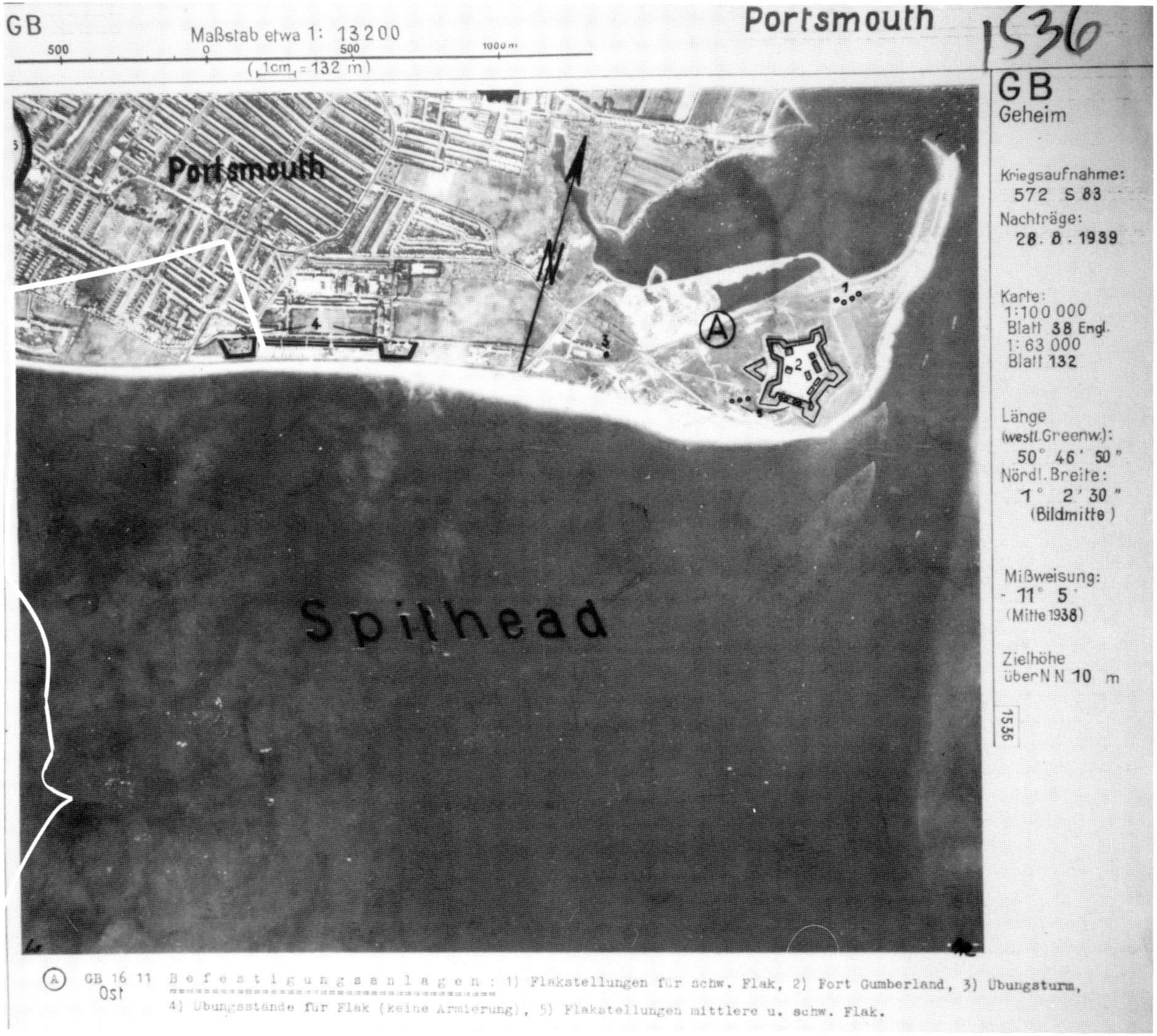

Portsmouth
28th September 1939
Fort Cumberland, Eastney and coastal Fortifications
TN 1536

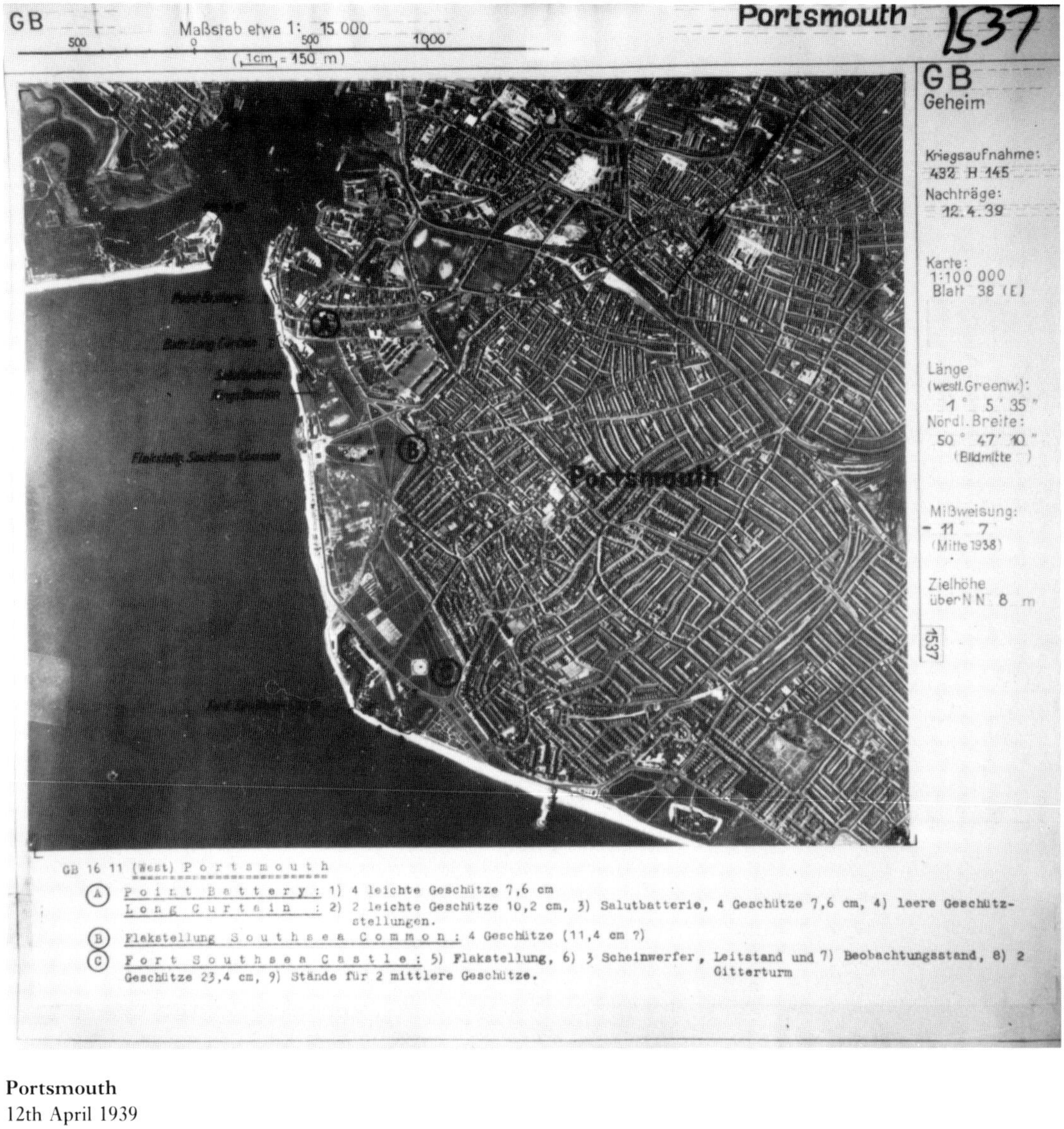

Portsmouth
12th April 1939
Fortifications TN 1537

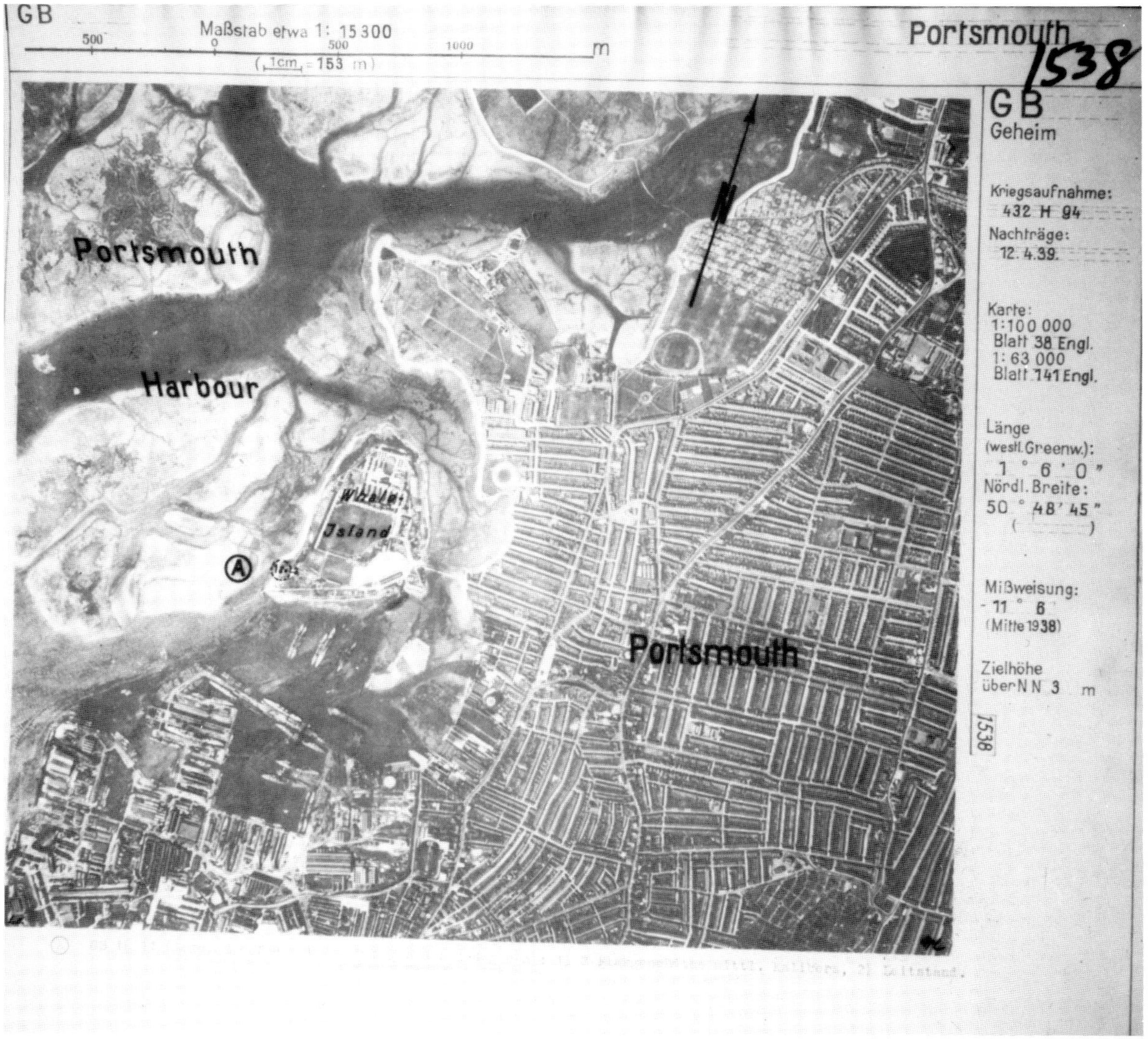

Portsmouth
12th April 1940
Whale Island, North End and Hilsea
TN 1538

Portsmouth
3rd September 1939
Fortifications
TN 1539

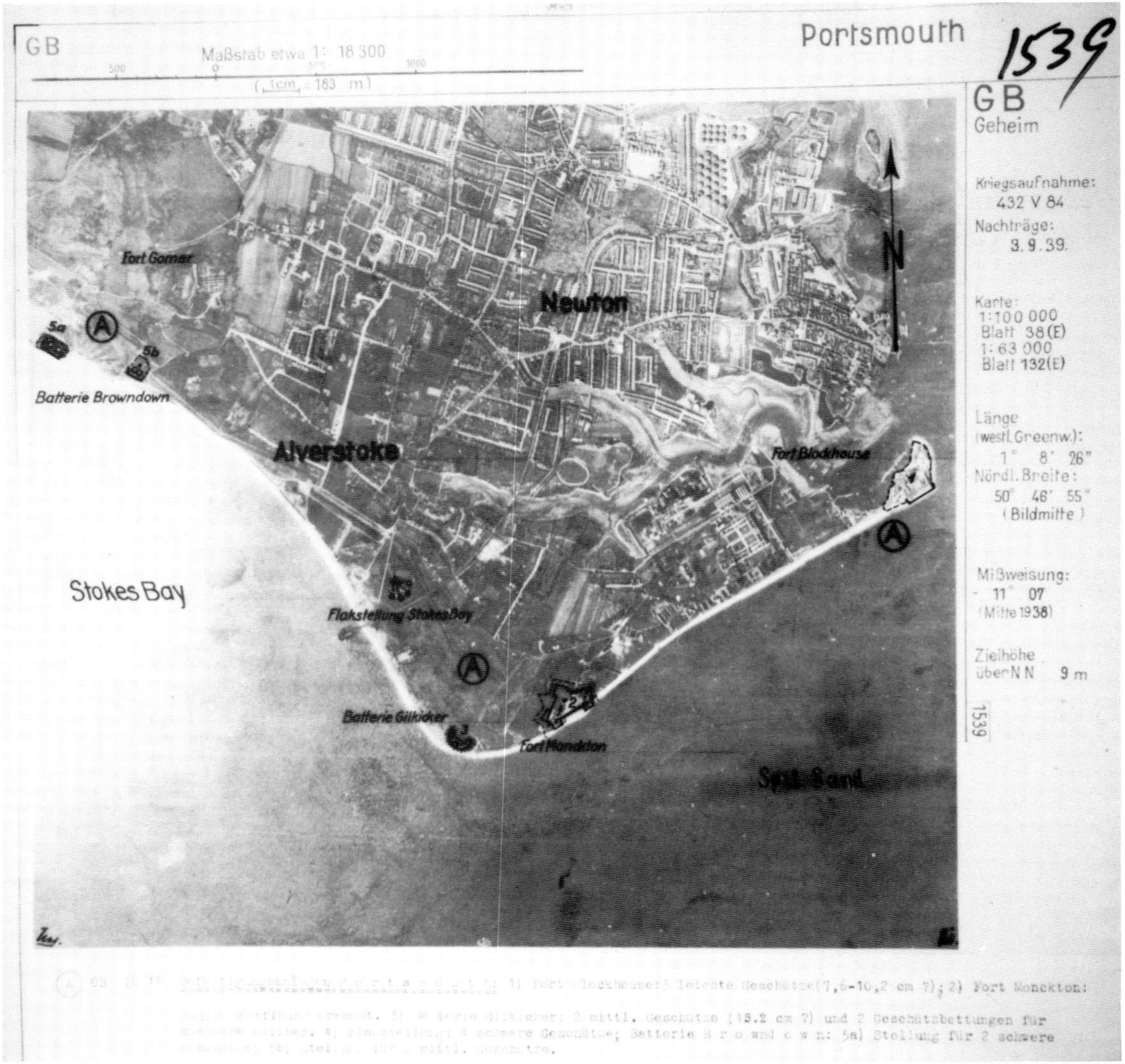

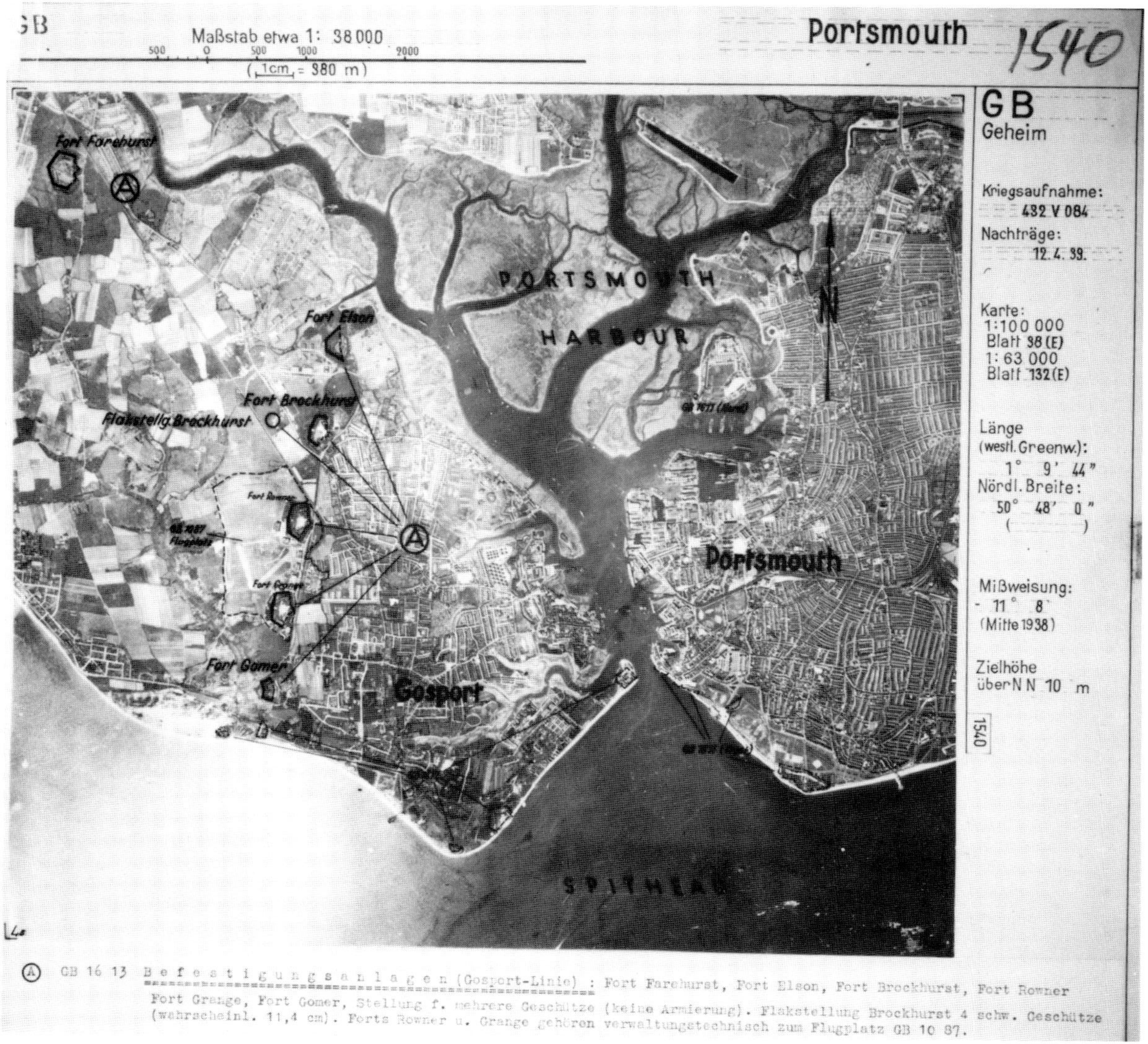

Portsmouth
12th April 1939
Gosport and Portsmouth
Fortifications
TN 1540

GB 10 205 **b c** **N. f. D.**	*Southampton–Eastleigh* *Flugplatz*	**Karte 1 : 100 000** **Engl. Bl.** 38 b

Bild Nr. 659 Z 10 **Geogr. Lage** 1° 21' **W,** 50° 57' **N, Höhe ü. d. M.** 11 **m** **Stand** X. 40

Maßstab etwa 1: 16 000 (1 cm = 160 m) Lfl. Kdo. 3

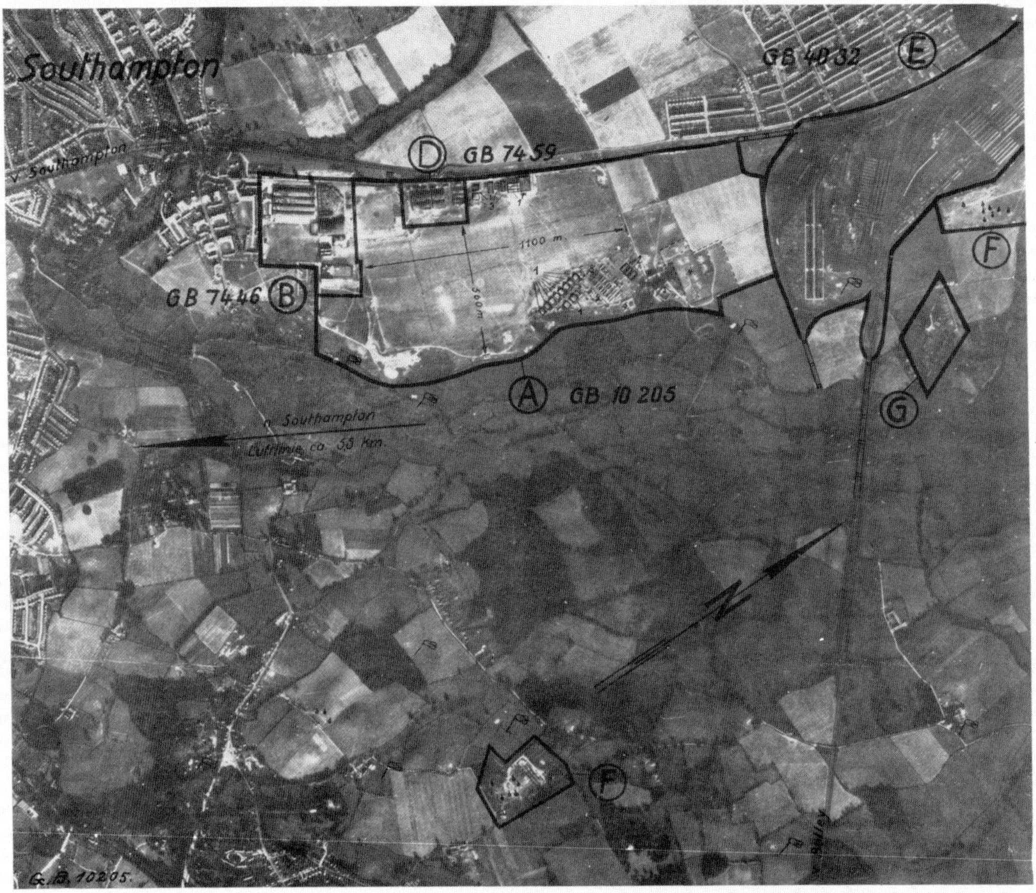

(A) GB 10 205 Flugplatz	1 100 x 560 m		
1) 12 Hallen	etwa	14 000 qm	
2) 3 Lagerhallen	etwa	3 600 qm	
3) Flugleitungs- und Werkstättengebäude	etwa	3 500 qm	
4) Munitionsschuppen	etwa	800 qm	
5) Unterkunfts- und Nebengebäude	etwa	4 500 qm	
bebaute Fläche	etwa	26 400 qm	

(B) GB 74 46 Flugzeugfab... der Supermarine Aviation Co.Ltd. (Vickers)

(D) GB 74 59 Reparaturwerkstätten v. A.V.Roe u.Co. Jersey Aircraft u.Vickers

(E) GB 40 32 Eastleigh (South.) Bahnanlagen und Werkstätten der Southern Ry.

(F) Flakstellungen

(G) Kläranlage

Southampton–Eastleigh

Eastleigh Airfield
GB 10205

GB 45 34 bc N. f. D.	**Southampton** *Kaianlage Südspitze*	Karte 1:100 000 Engl. Bl. 38b

Bild Nr. 359 Z 45 **Geogr. Lage** 1°23' W, 50°54' N, **Höhe ü. d. M.** — m Stand VIII. 40.

Maßstab etwa 1: 16 500 (1 cm = 165 m)

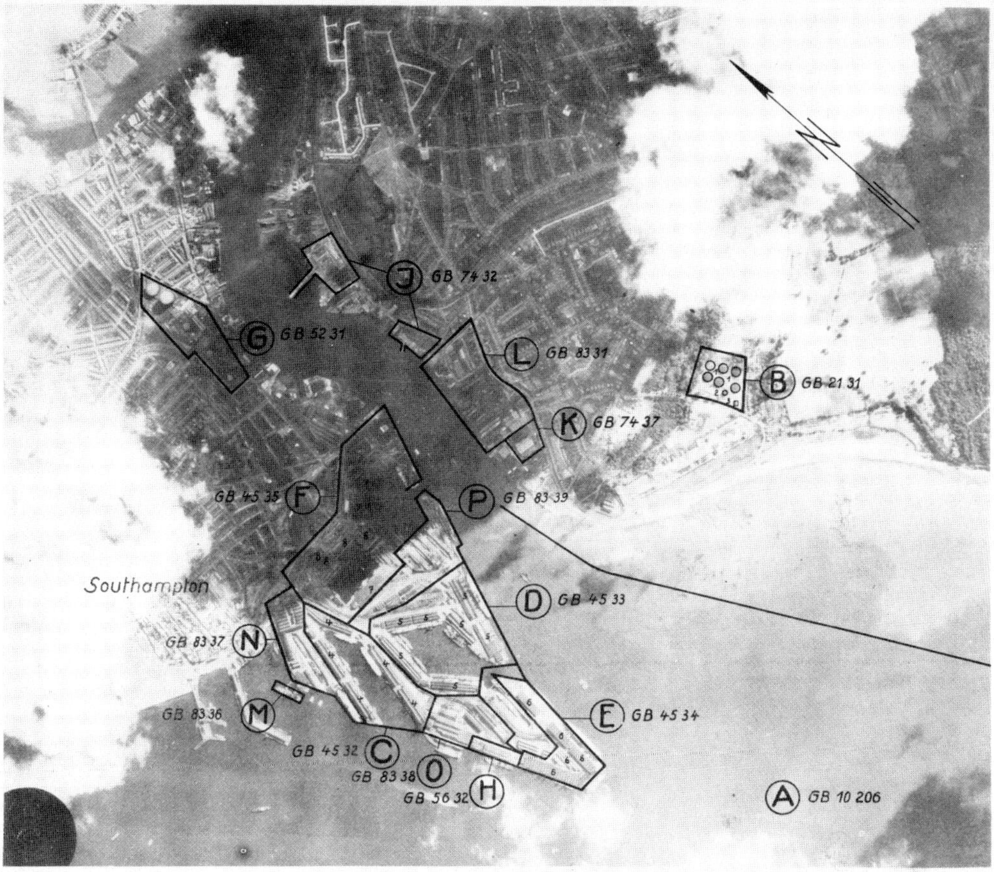

(A) GB 10 206 Flugplatz Southampton (Woolston-Hythe)

(B) GB 21 31 Tanklager Woolston(South.)
1) 6 Tanks ca. 40 m Ø
2) 1 Tank ca. 25 m Ø
3) Pumpstation

(C) GB 45 32 Ocean Dock
4) 5 Lagerhallen 570x25m (14 000qm)

(D) GB 45 33 Kaianlagen am Empress Dock
5) 7 Lagerhallen 1350x35m (47 000qm)

(E) GB 45 34 Kaianlagen a.d.Südspitze
6) 5 Lagerhallen 850x35m (3o 000qm)

(F) GB 45 35 Innen-und Aussendock
7) 3 Lagerhallen 550x35m (19 000qm)
8) 4 Getreidespeicher 380x35m (13 000qm)

(G) GB 52 31 Hauptgaswerk

(H) GB 56 32 Kühlhaus Southampton

(I) GB 74 32 Flugzeugfabrik Southampton-Woolston
Supermarine Aviation Works

(K) GB 74 37 Flugzeugfabrik Southampton-Woolston
Neue Fabrik A.V.Roe u.Co.

(L) GB 83 31 Woolston(South.)Werft
d.John I.Thornycroft u.Co.Ltd.

(M) GB 83 36 Grosses Schwimmdock

(N) GB 83 37 Trafalgar Trockendock

(O) GB 83 38 Prince of Wales Trockendock

(P) GB 83 39 4 Trockendocks im Aussendock

Southampton

Docks
GB4534

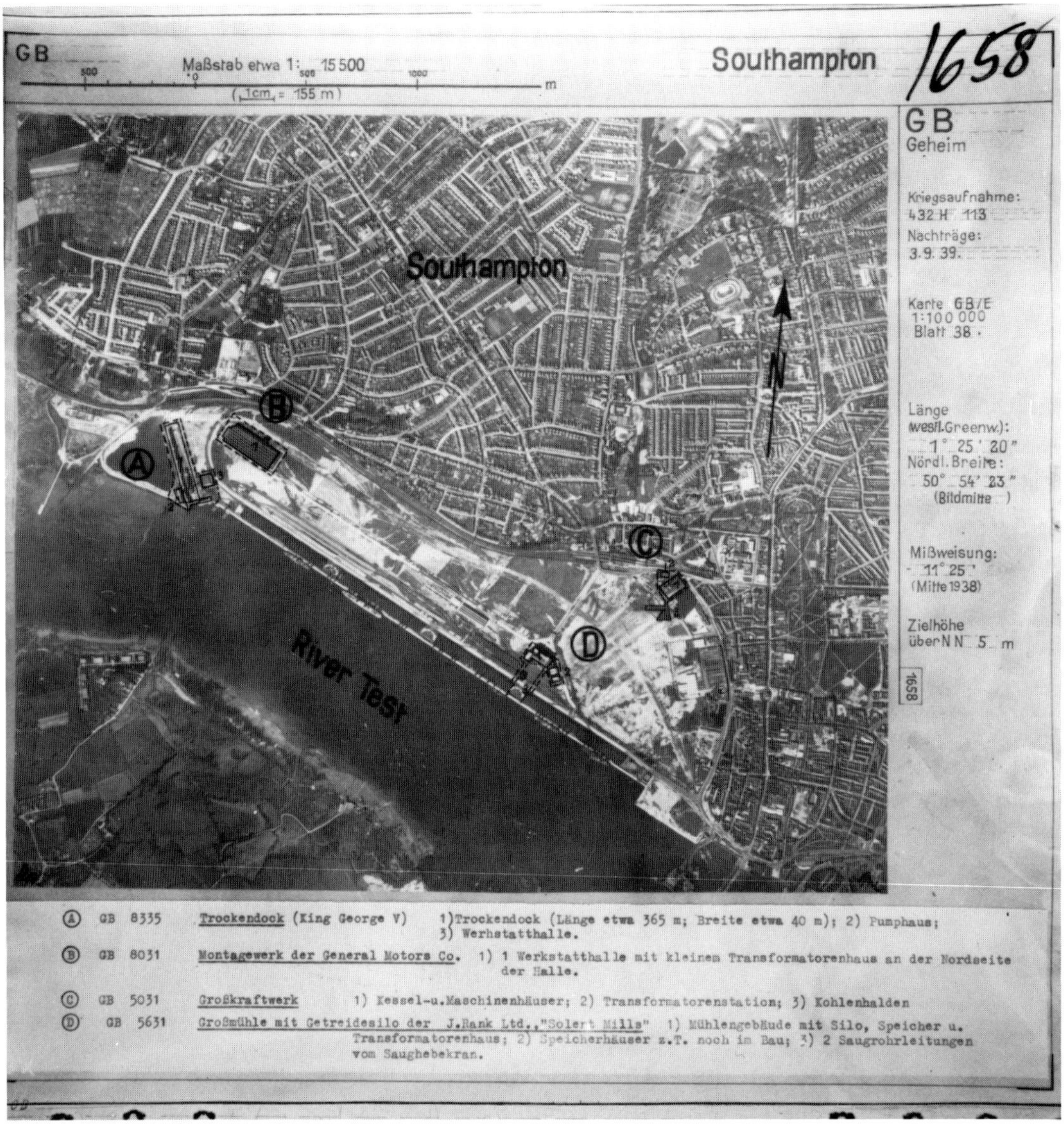

Southampton
3rd September 1939
Docks, mills, grain silos. General Motors assembly works
TN 1658

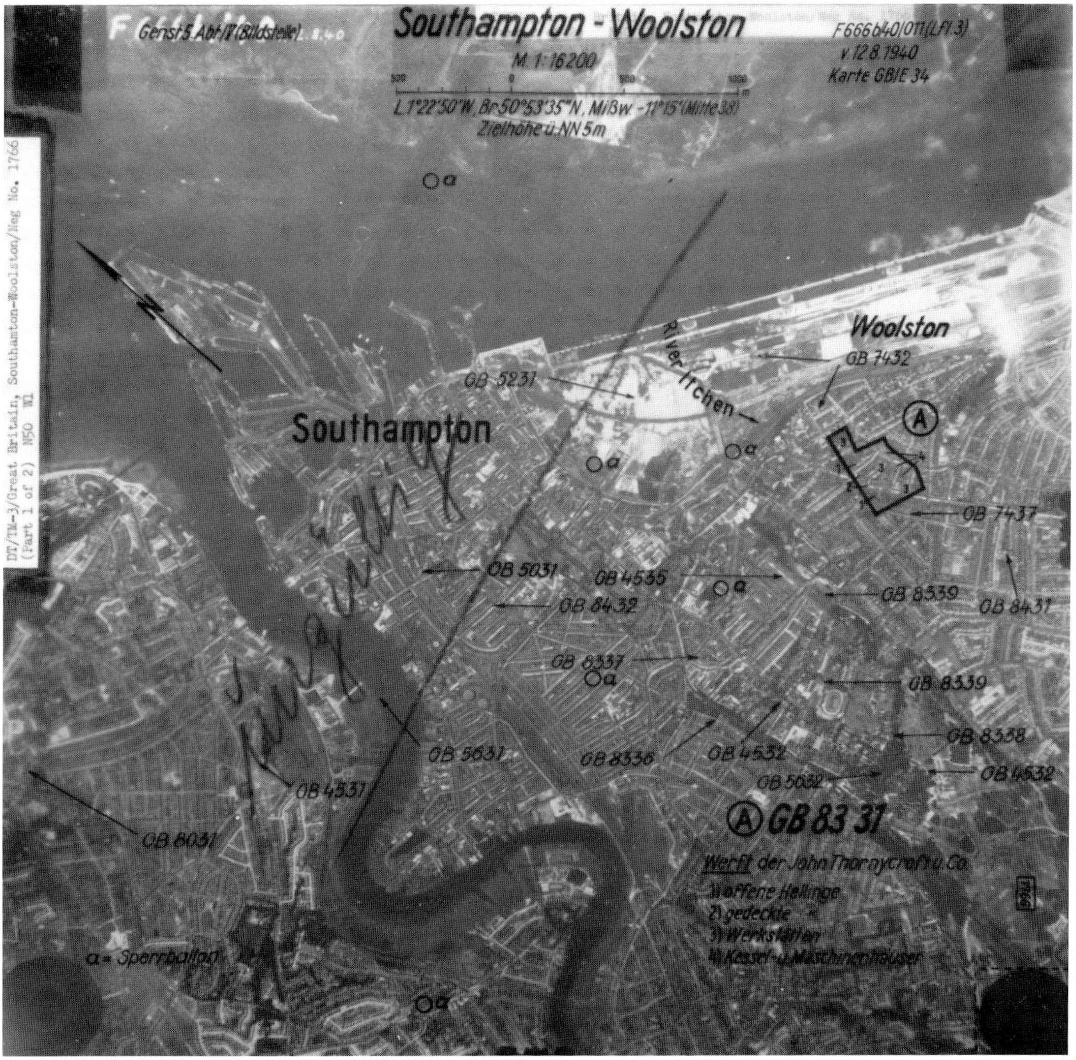

Southampton
12th August 1940
Thorneycroft Marine Works
TN 1766

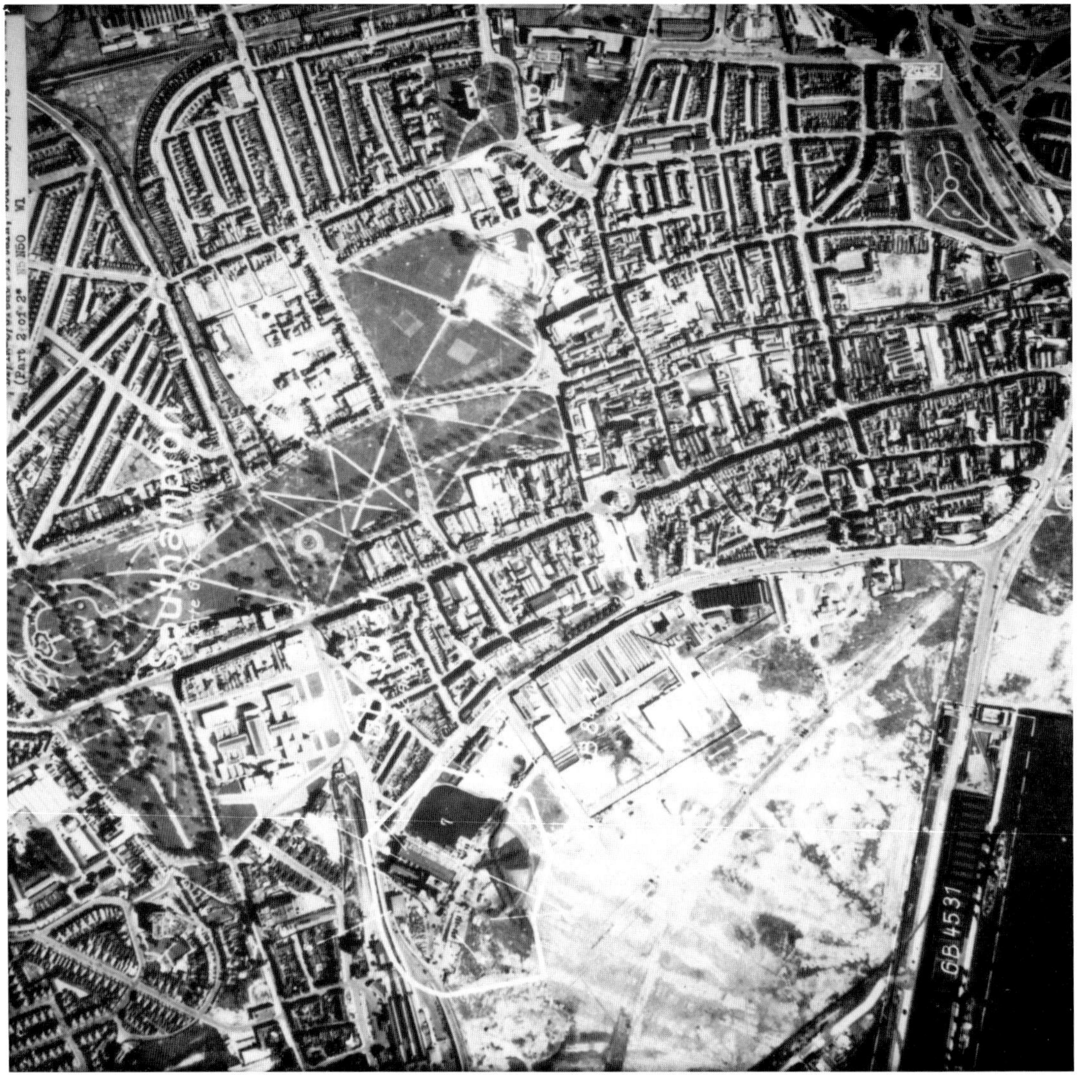

Southampton

Power Station
TN 2412

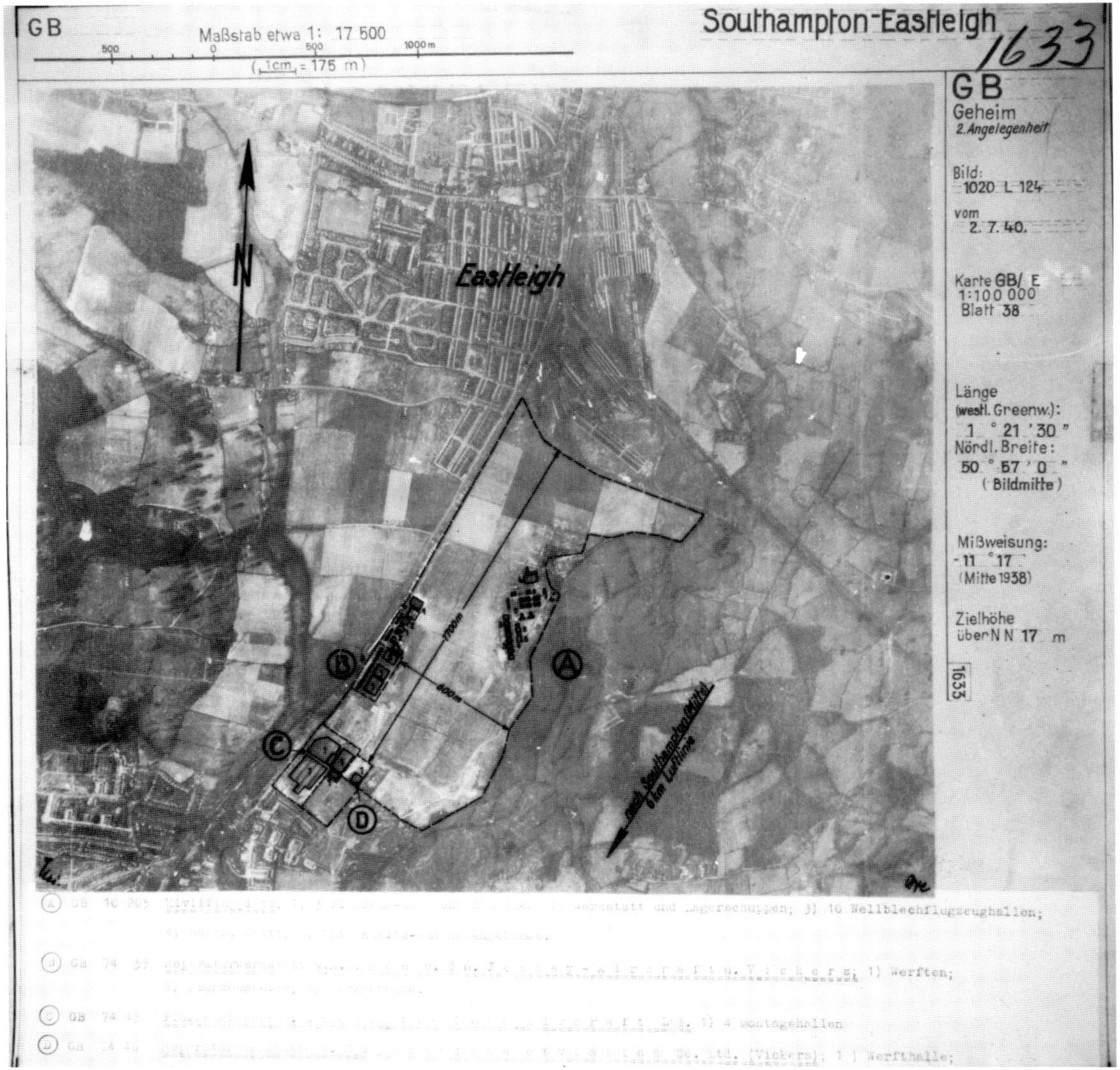

Southampton–Eastleigh
2nd July 1940
Eastleigh Airfield
TN 1633

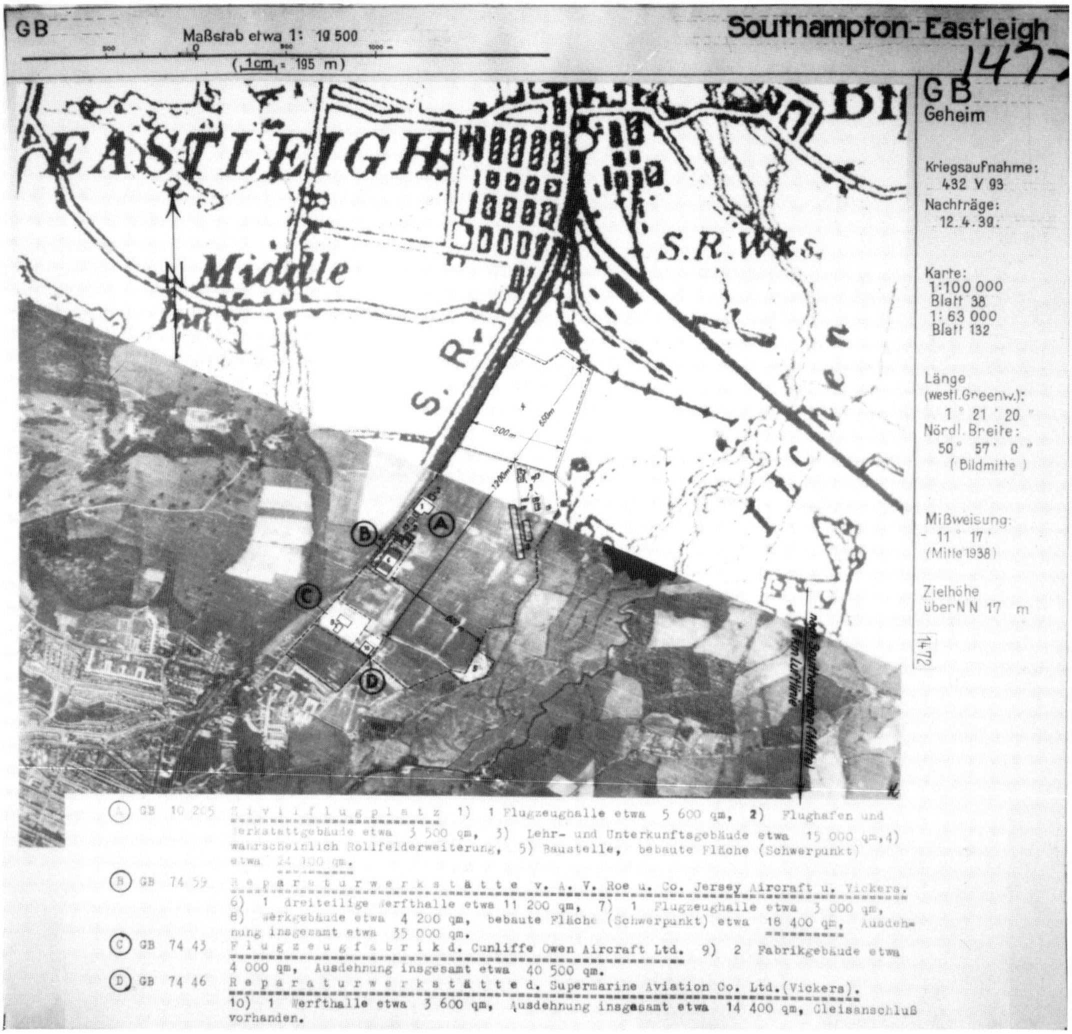

Southampton–Eastleigh
12th March 1939
Eastleigh Airfield
TN 1472

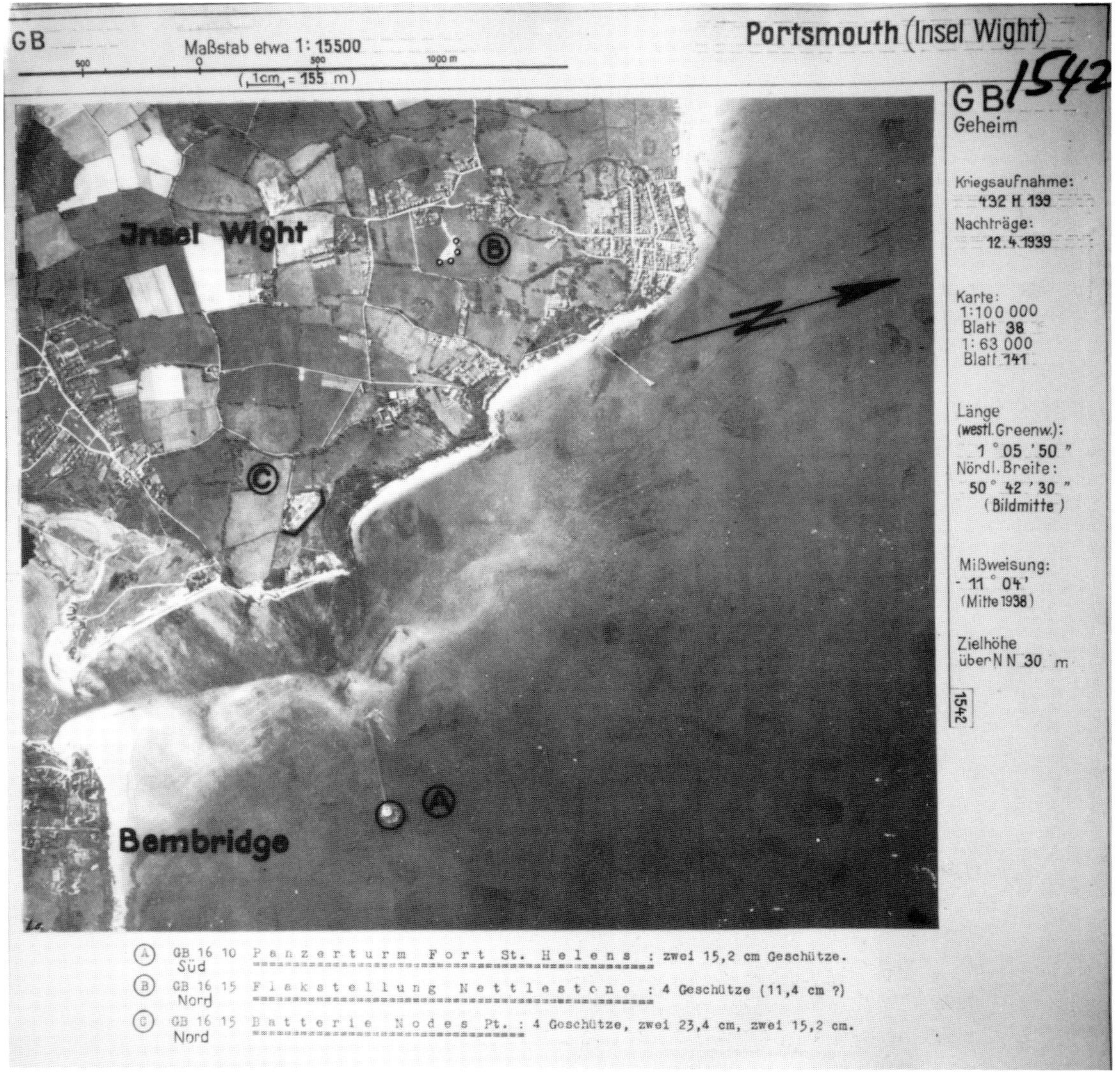

Bembridge
14th April 1939
Bembridge, fortifications and wireless station.
TN 1542

ISLE OF WIGHT

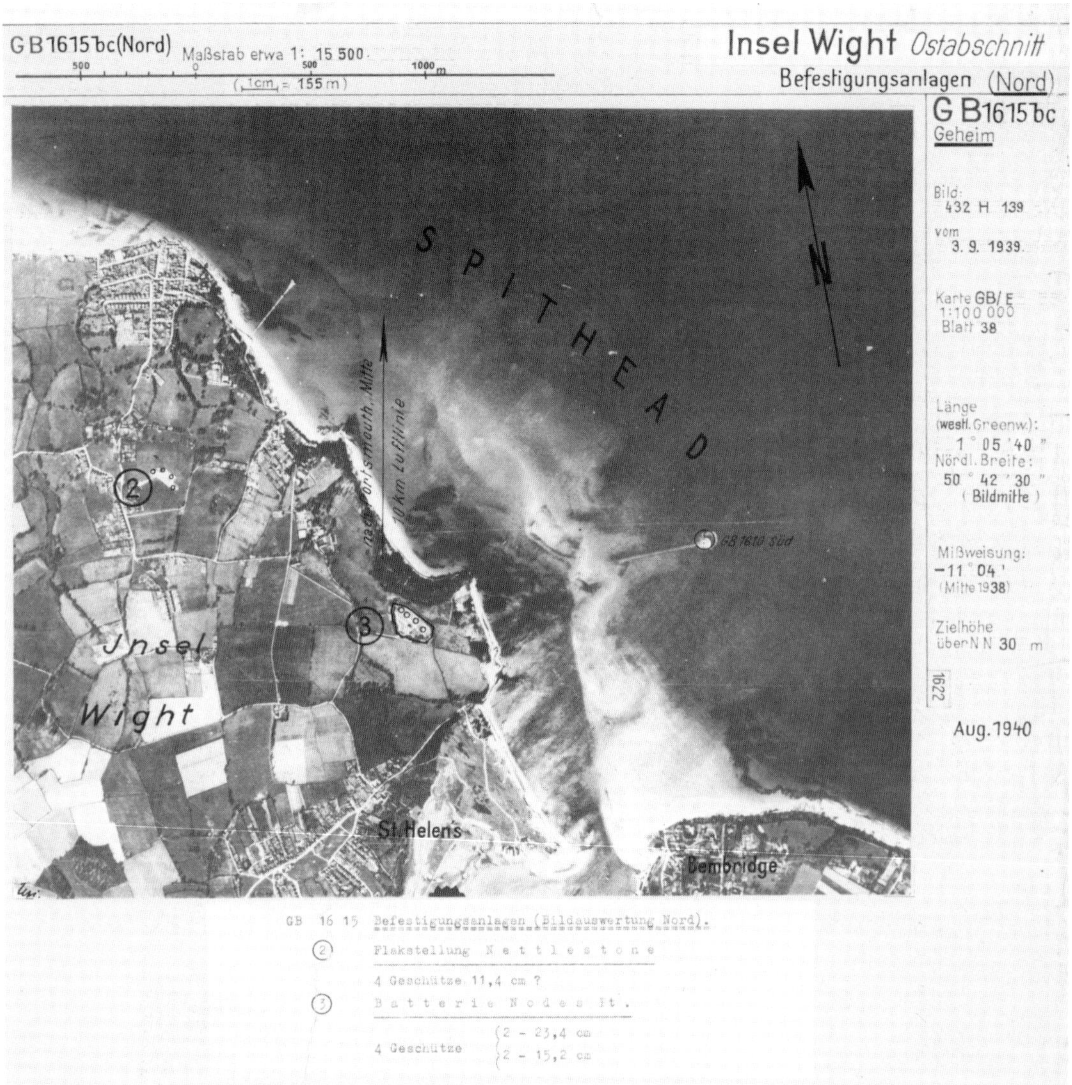

Bembridge
3rd September 1939
Bembridge fortifications
TN 1622

Cowes
28th July 1940
Cowes, Samuel White aircraft factory
TN 1650

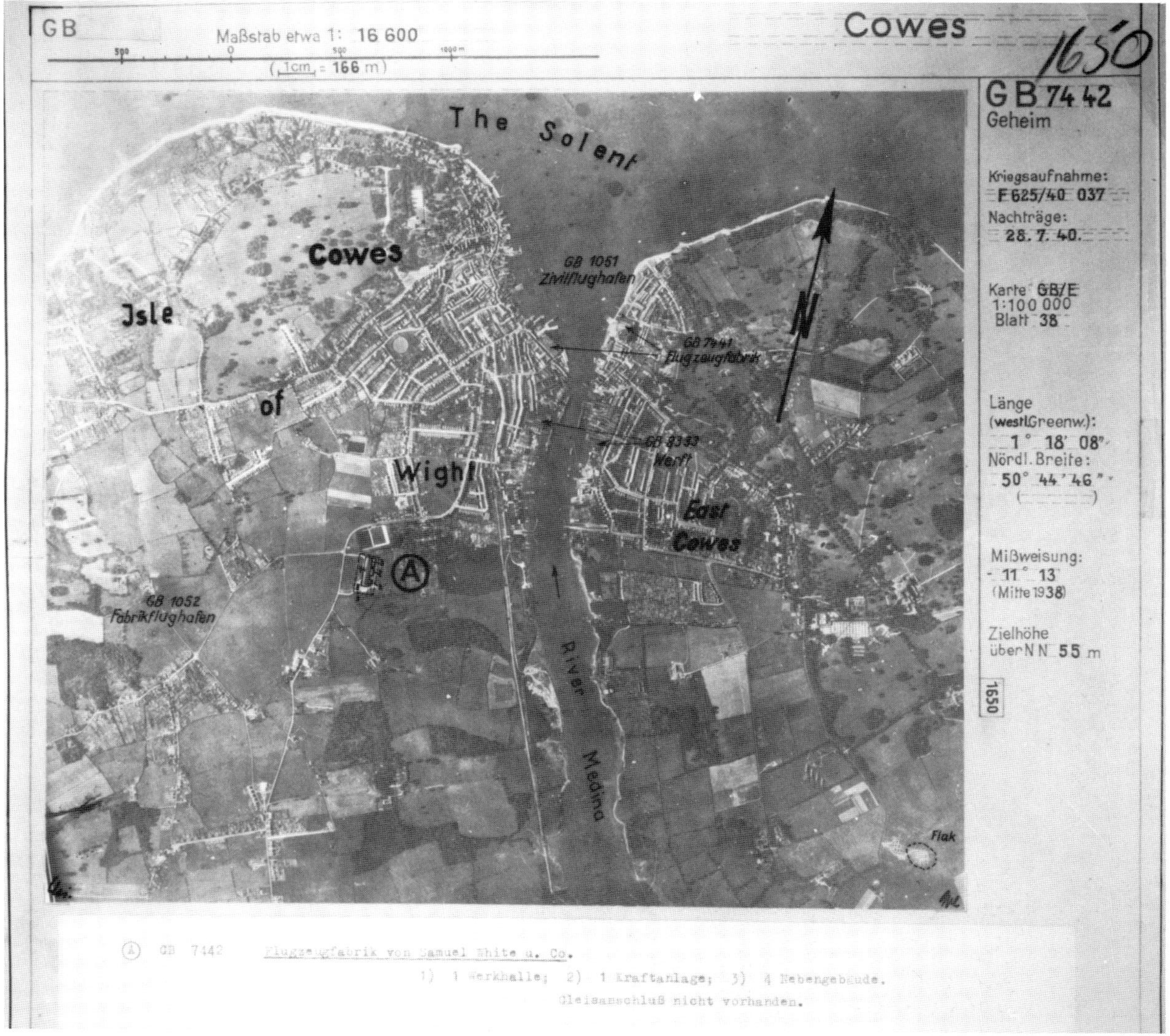

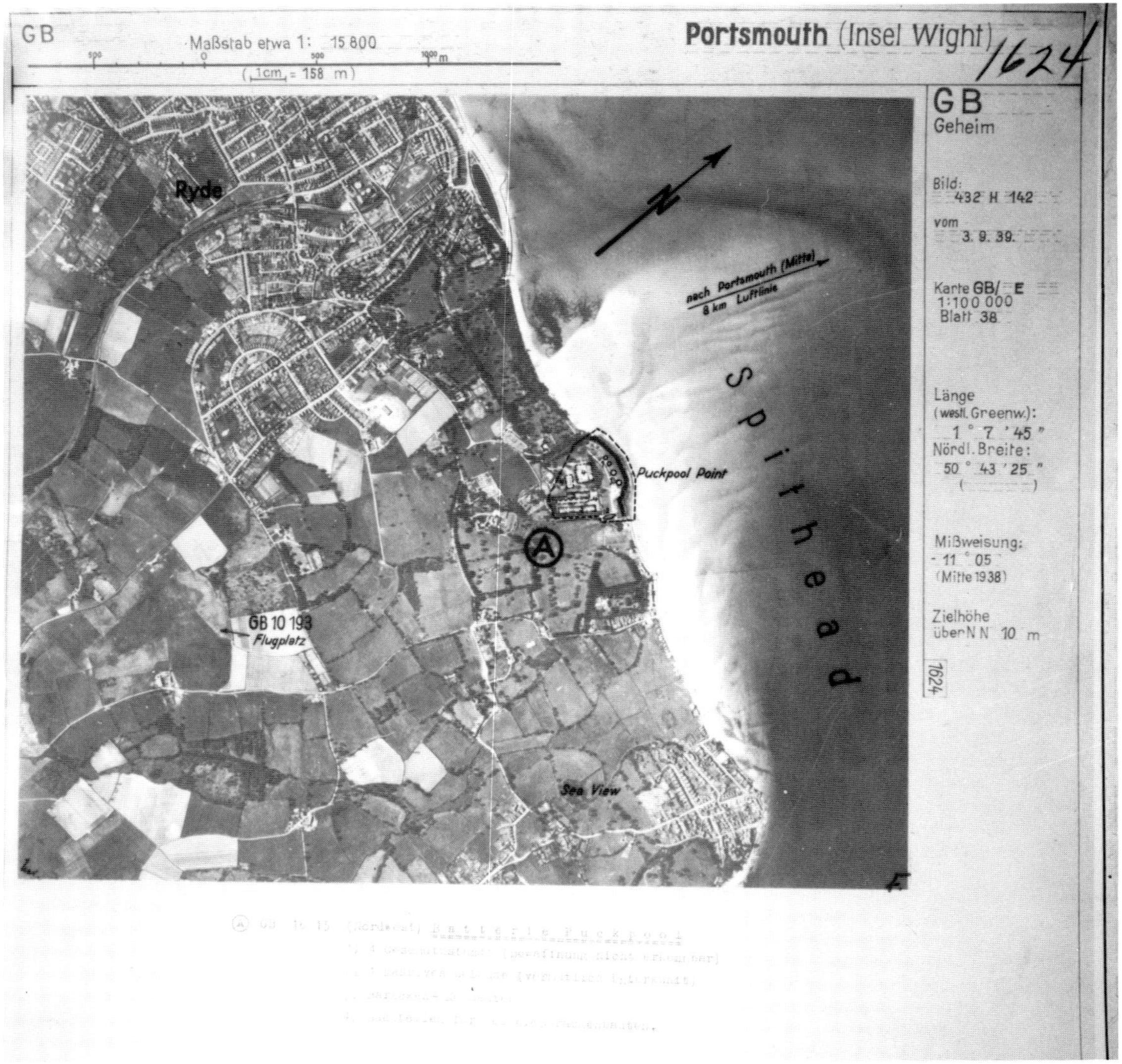

Ryde
3rd September 1939
HMS Medina Fleet Air Arm training base and barracks
TN 1624

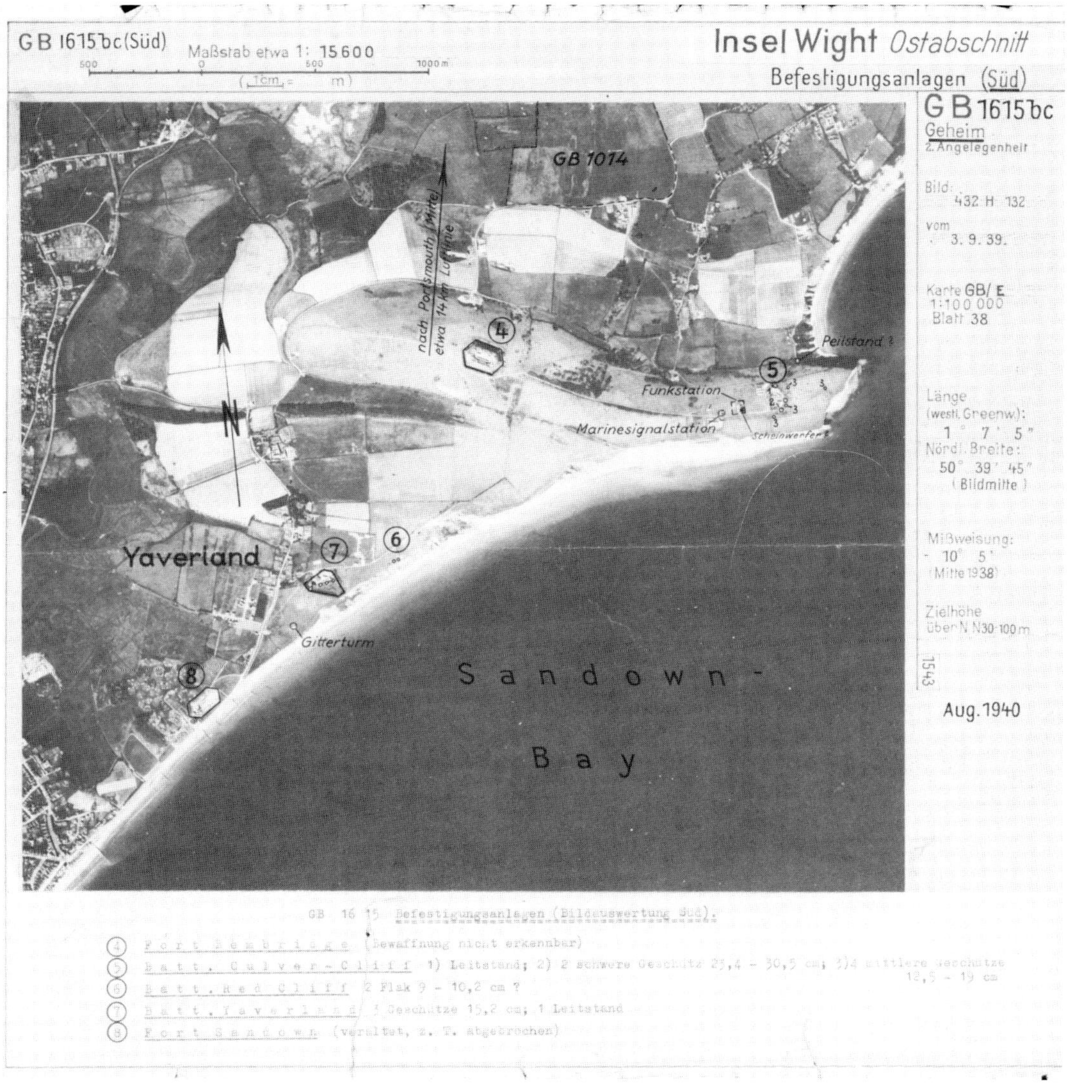

Culver Cliffs
3rd September 1939
Fortifications, Bembridge, Yaverland and Sandown
TN 1543

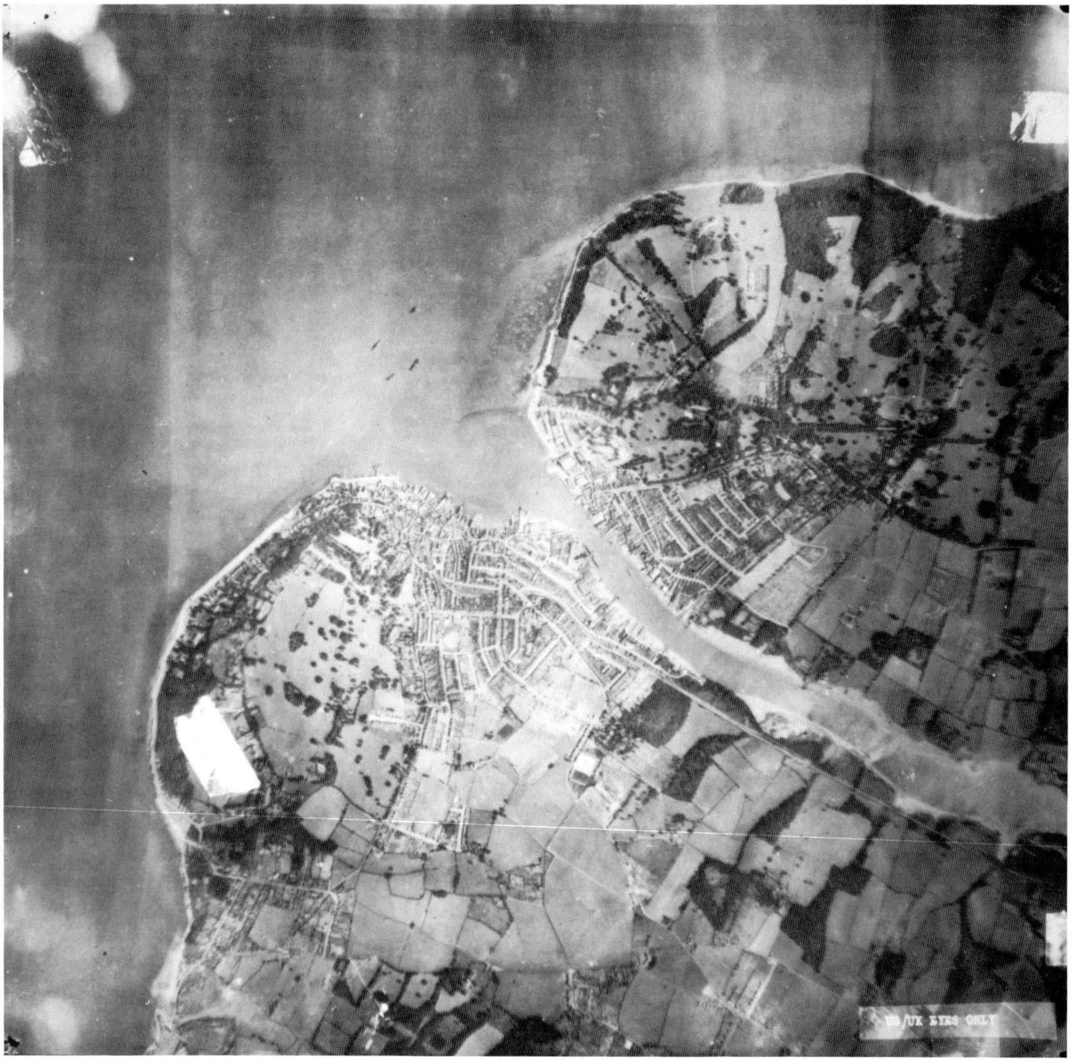

Isle of Wight
3rd September 1939
TN 1612

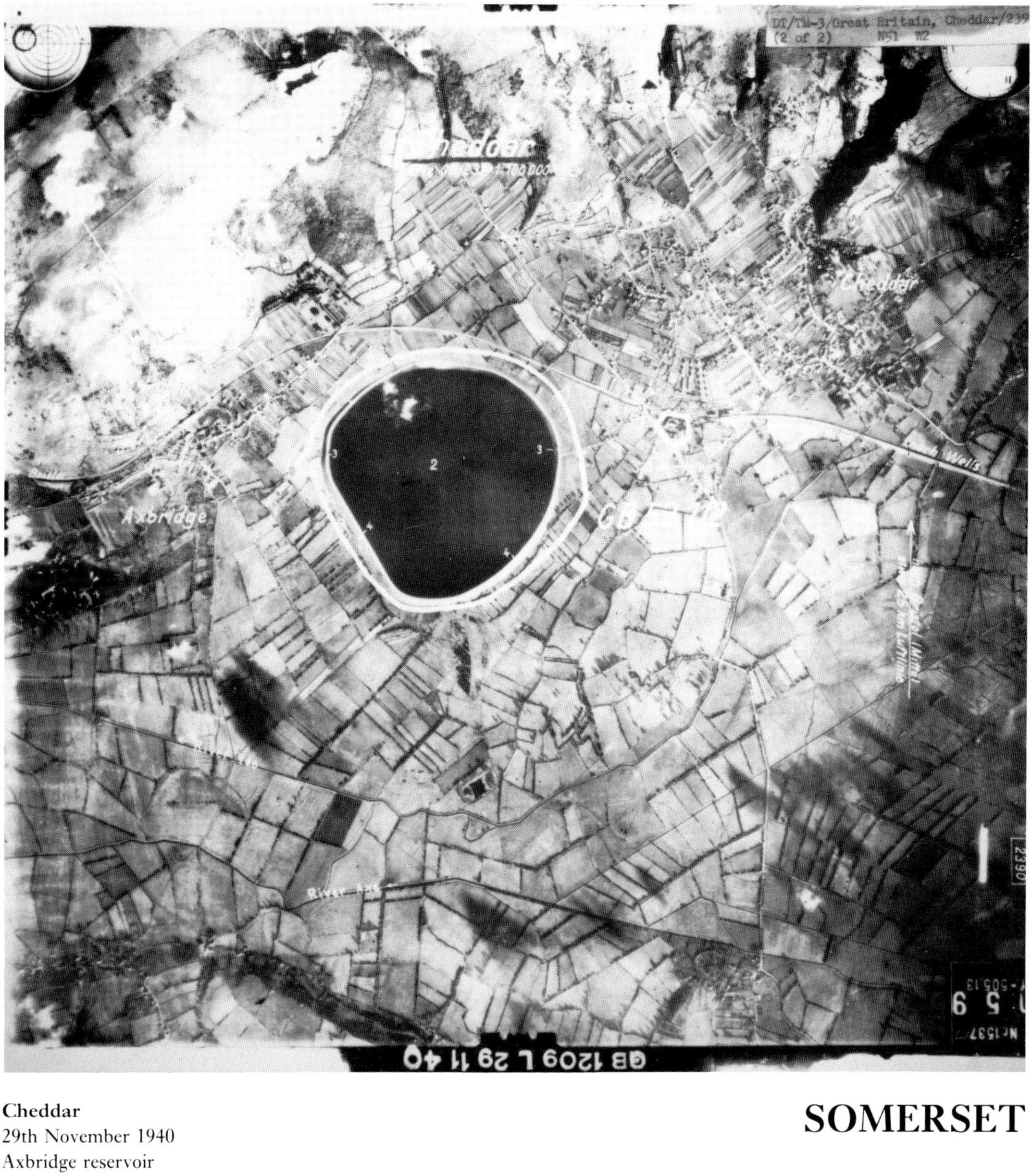

Cheddar
29th November 1940
Axbridge reservoir
TN 2390
Comment
In the top right side of the photograph can be seen the dark shadow of Cheddar Gorge.

SOMERSET

GB 23 5 bc **N. f. D.**	*Taunton* *Nachschublager*	**Karte 1 : 100 000** **Engl. Bl.** 32 c

Bild Nr. 258/40/005 **Geogr. Lage** 3° 08' W, 51° 01'30" N, **Höhe ü. d. M.** 35 m **Stand** X. 40

Maßstab etwa 1: 9500 (1 cm = 95 m) Lfl. Kdo. 3

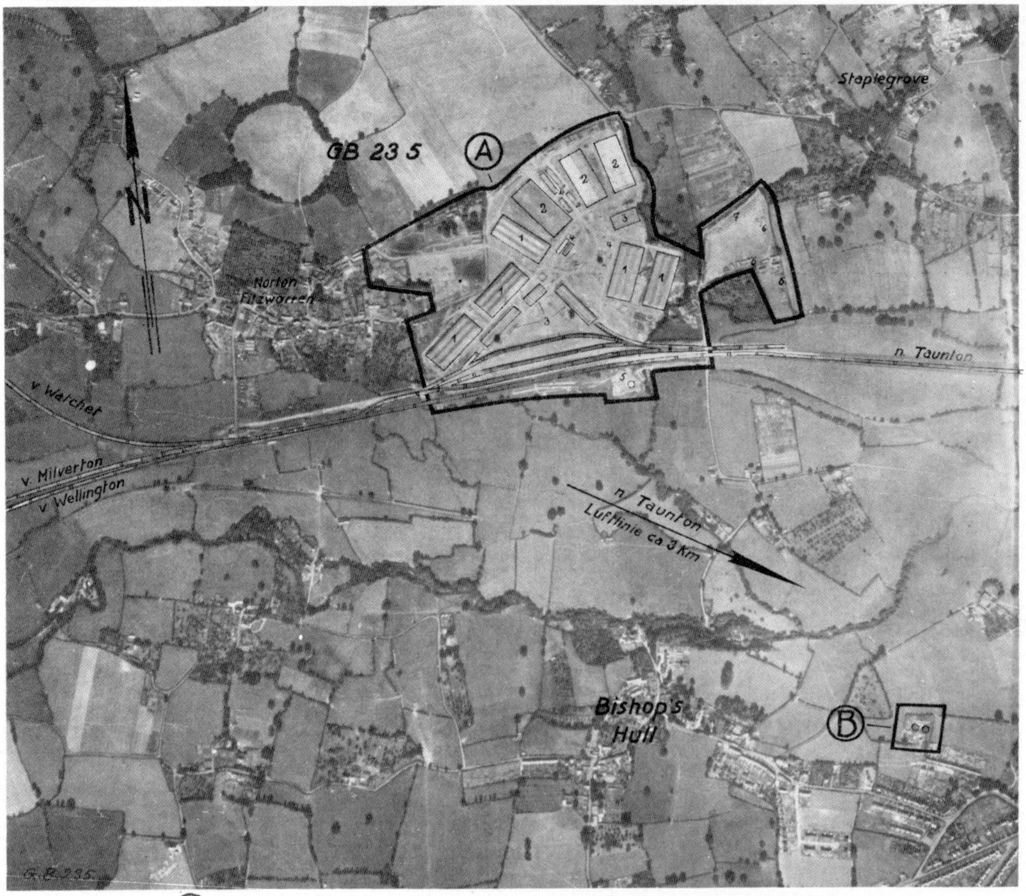

Ⓐ GB 23 5 Nachschublager des Heeres

1)	5 Hallen	etwa	42 500 qm
2)	3 Hallen im Bau	etwa	24 750 qm
3)	4 kleine Hallen im Bau	etwa	6 500 qm
4)	Lagergebäude im Bau	etwa	2 000 qm
5)	Kläranlage im Bau		
6)	12 Hauszelte	etwa	300 qm
7)	68 Rundzelte	etwa	250 qm
	bebaute Fläche	etwa	76 300 qm
	gesamte Fläche	etwa	360 000 qm

Ⓑ Kläranlage

Taunton
1940
Barracks
GB 23 5

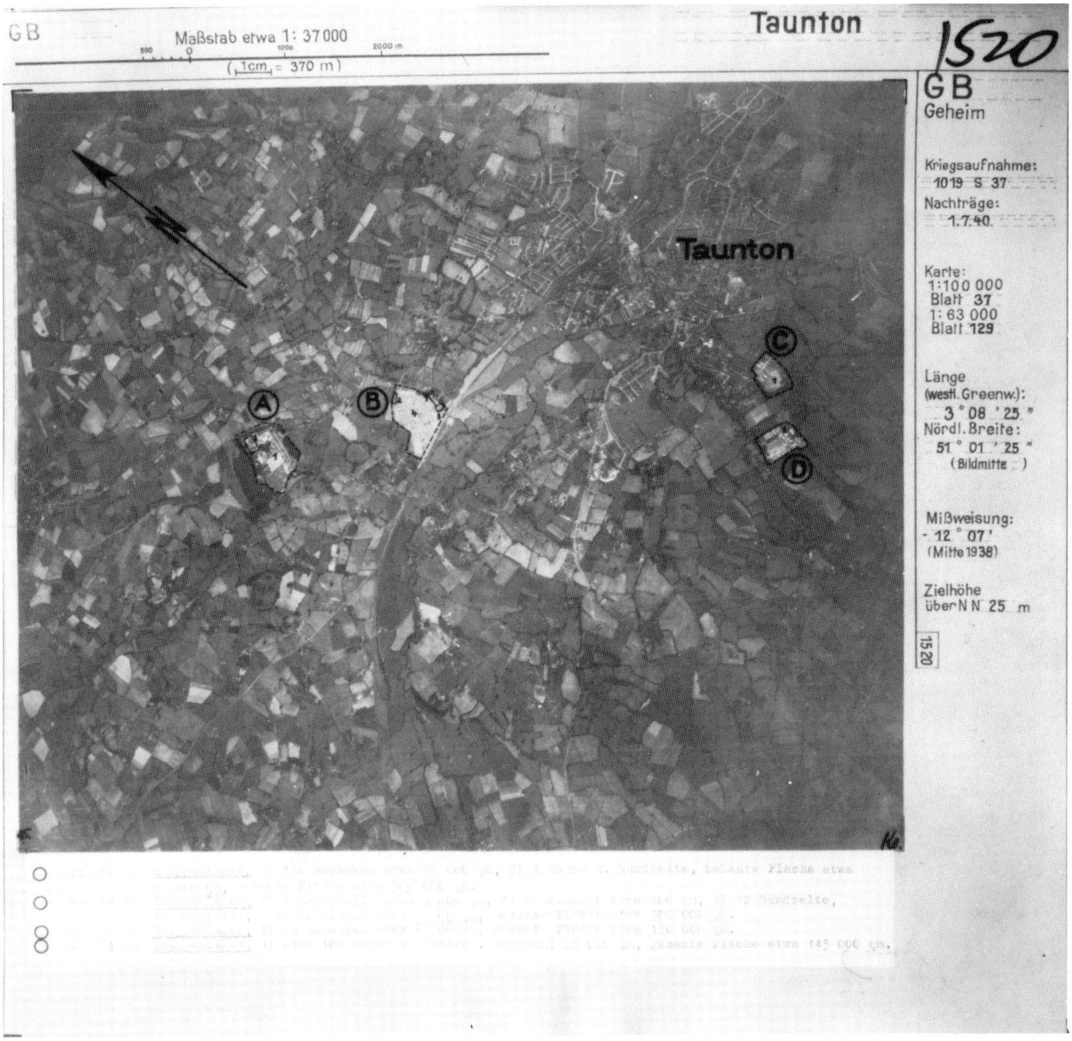

Taunton
1st July 1940
Wireless Station
TN 1520
Comment
In the last fifty years Taunton has grown, the motorway passes to the east of the town and new housing and industrial estates have been constructed. The town is thought to date from about the eleventh century and has always been an important market centre serving a large farming and rural community.

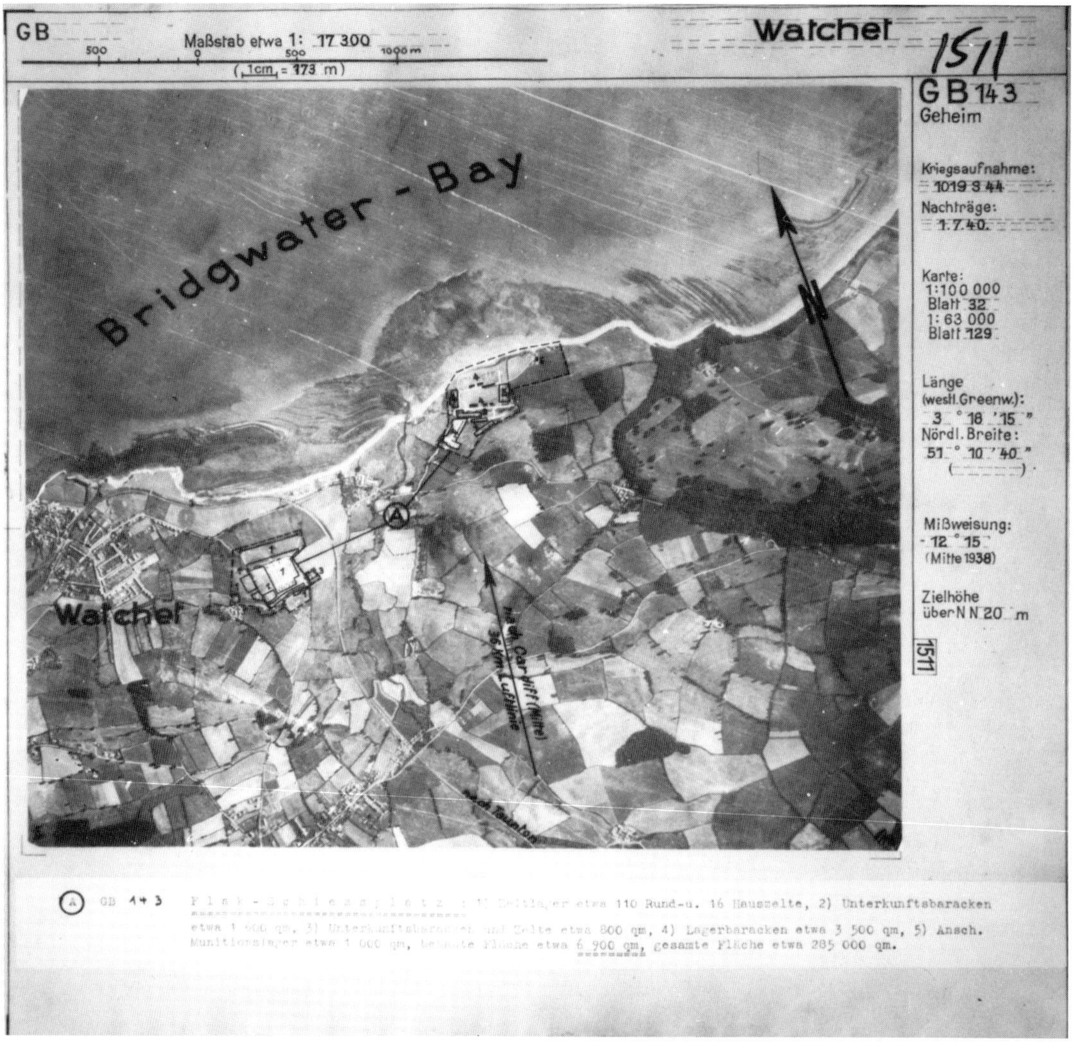

Watchet
1st July 1940
Anti-aircraft gun training area
TN 1511
Comment
Doriford camp near Watchet was one of the main training camps for ack-ack training. The Watchet ranges were used till the late 1950's. Today the only trace of the camp is the concrete base of the gun park. The town of Watchet dates back to the middle ages. The harbour was developed for the loading of iron ore from the near-by Brendon Hill mines, during the nineteenth century.

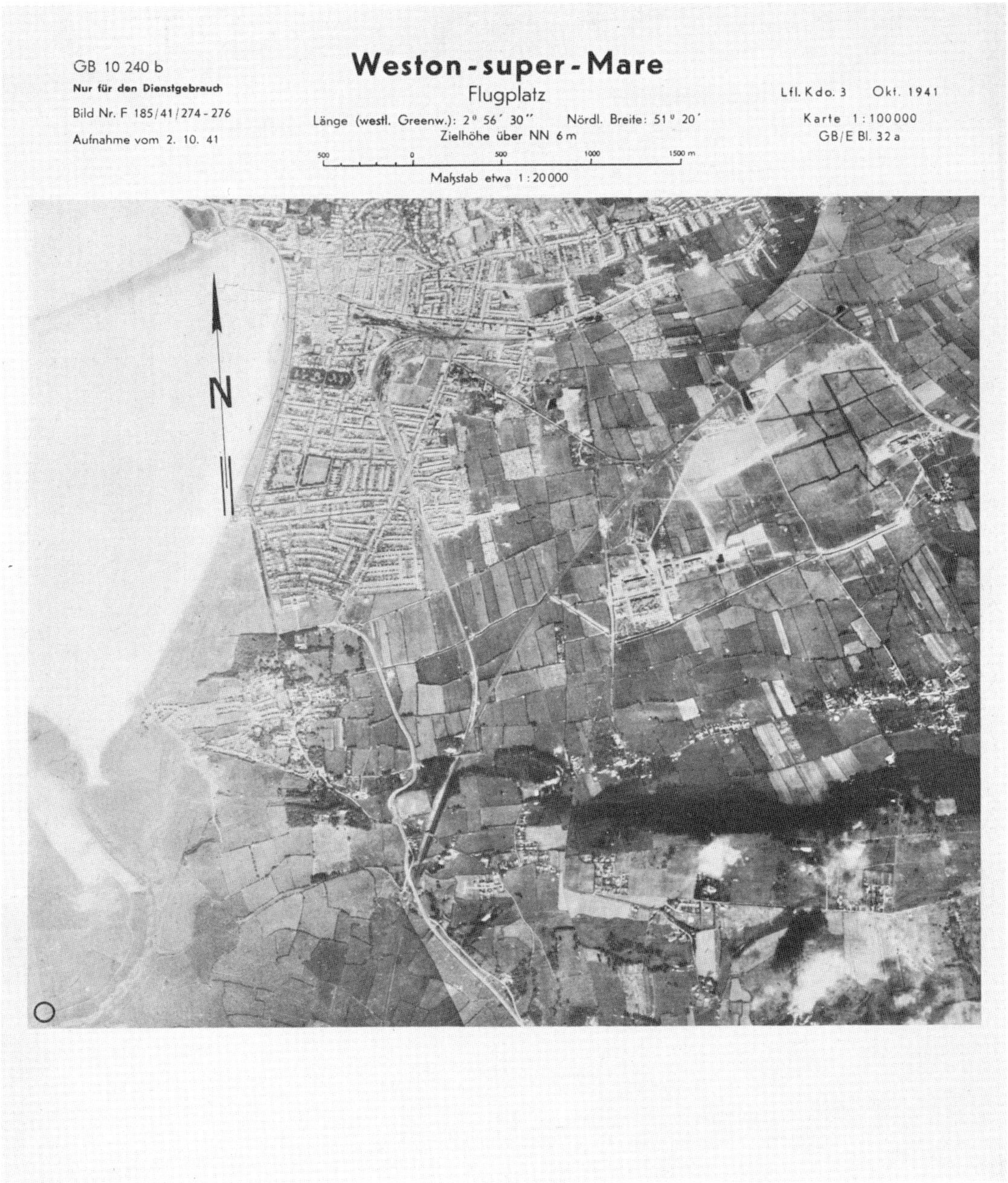

Weston-Super-Mare
2nd October 1941
Airfield
GB 10240
Comment

The airfield at Weston-Super-Mare was originally constructed for civilian flights in 1936 and then transferred to the RAF in 1940. Two shadow factories were constructed at Hutton and Old Mixon, by the Bristol Aeroplane Company for the production of Beauforts and Beaufighters. The site of the airfield has now been sold to developers and while the runway still exits much of the peripheral land has gone to housing and industrial development.

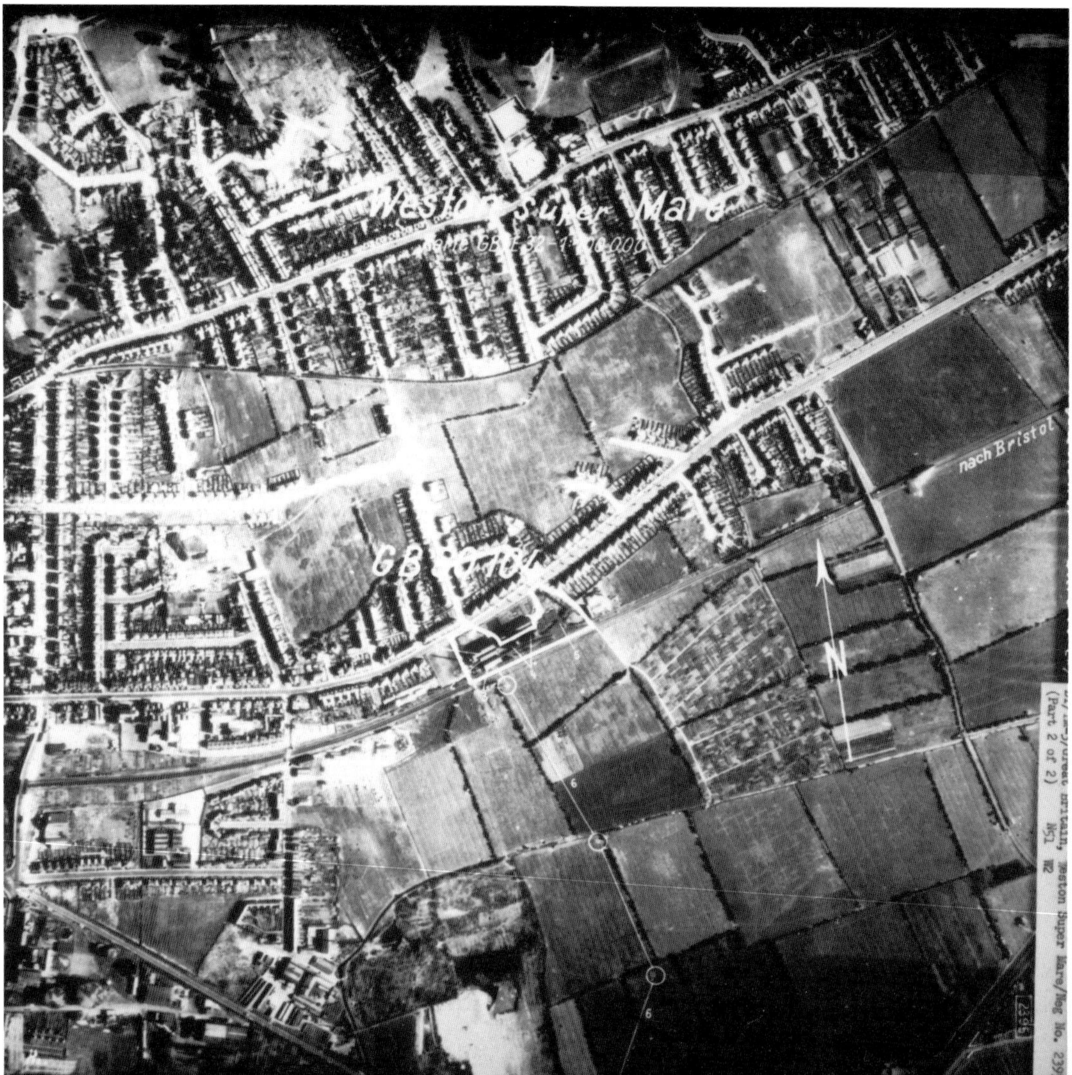

Weston-Super-Mare
24th August 1940
Electricity sub station
TN 2395
Comment
The Bristol Aeroplane Company had a factory in Weston-Super-Mare. The town was heavily bombed in 1942 on the nights of the 28th and 29th of June.

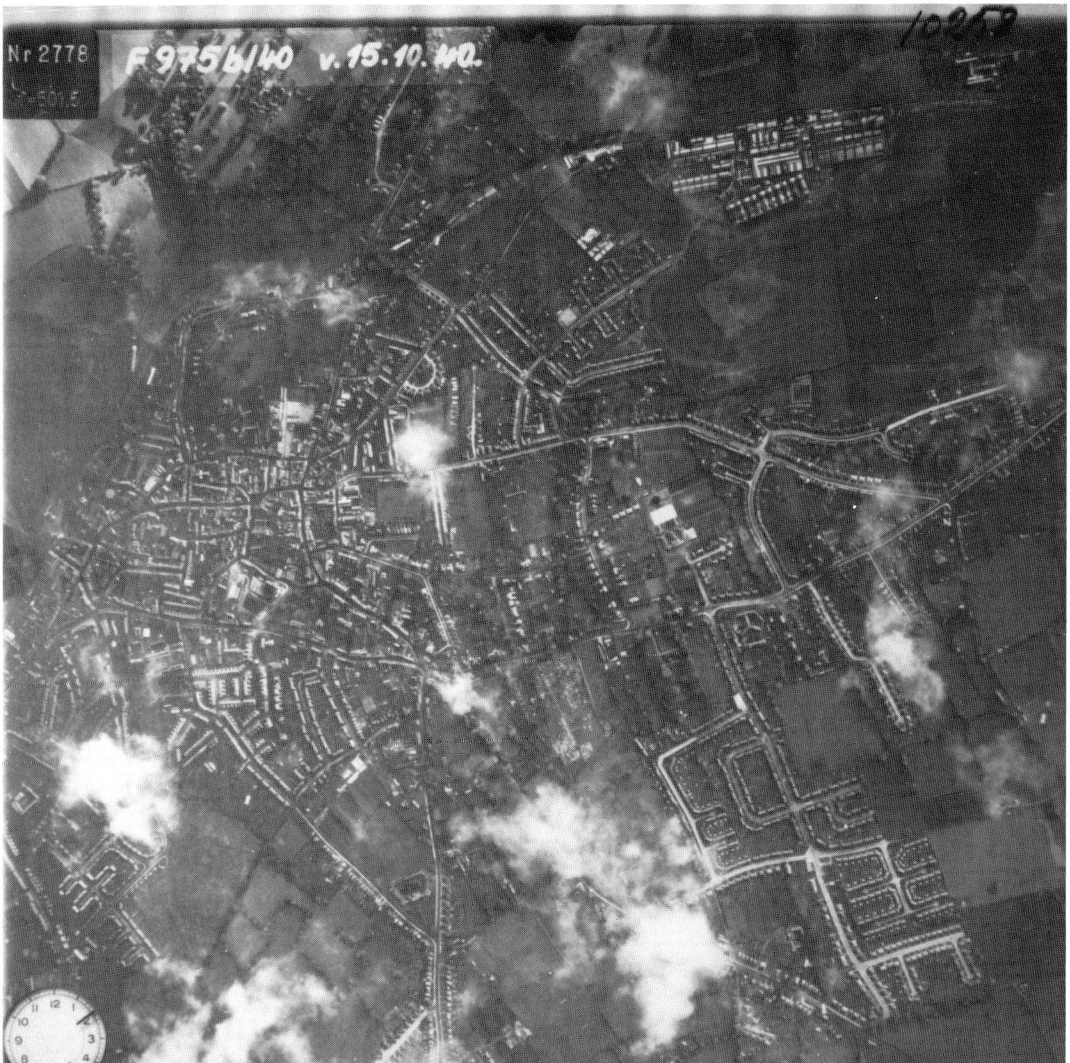

Yeovil
15th October 1940
Westland aircraft works
TN 10258
Comment
The airfield has been camouflaged as fields and if you look carefully at the photograph you can see barrage balloons above the perimeter of the airfield.

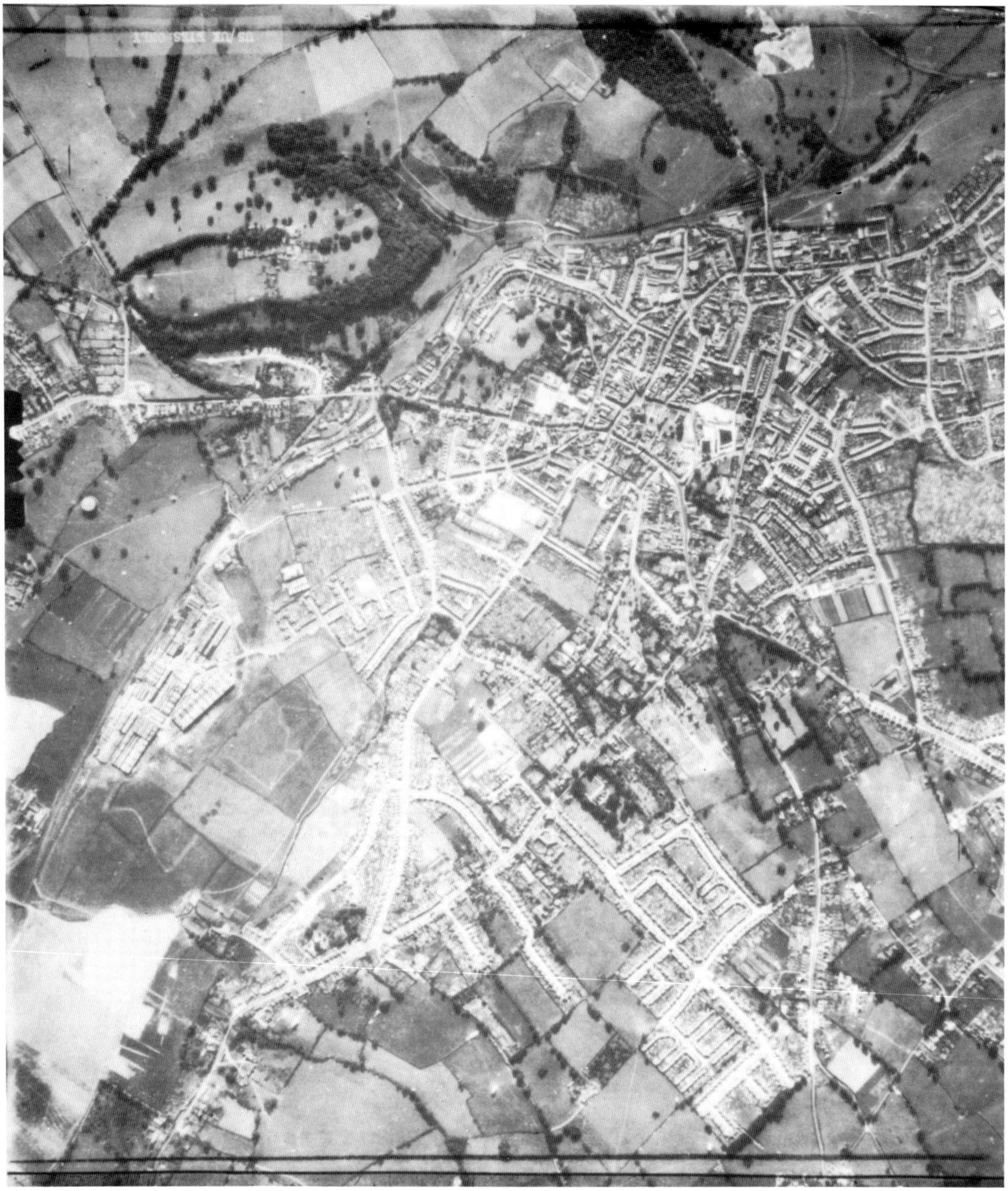

Yeovil

GX 10258 015
Town centre
Comment
Yeovil in 1940 was dominated by the Westland Aircraft works and the factory still occupies the same site, though greatly enlarged. The old Yeovil town pitch is now the site of a supermarket and the ring road now cuts through the town.

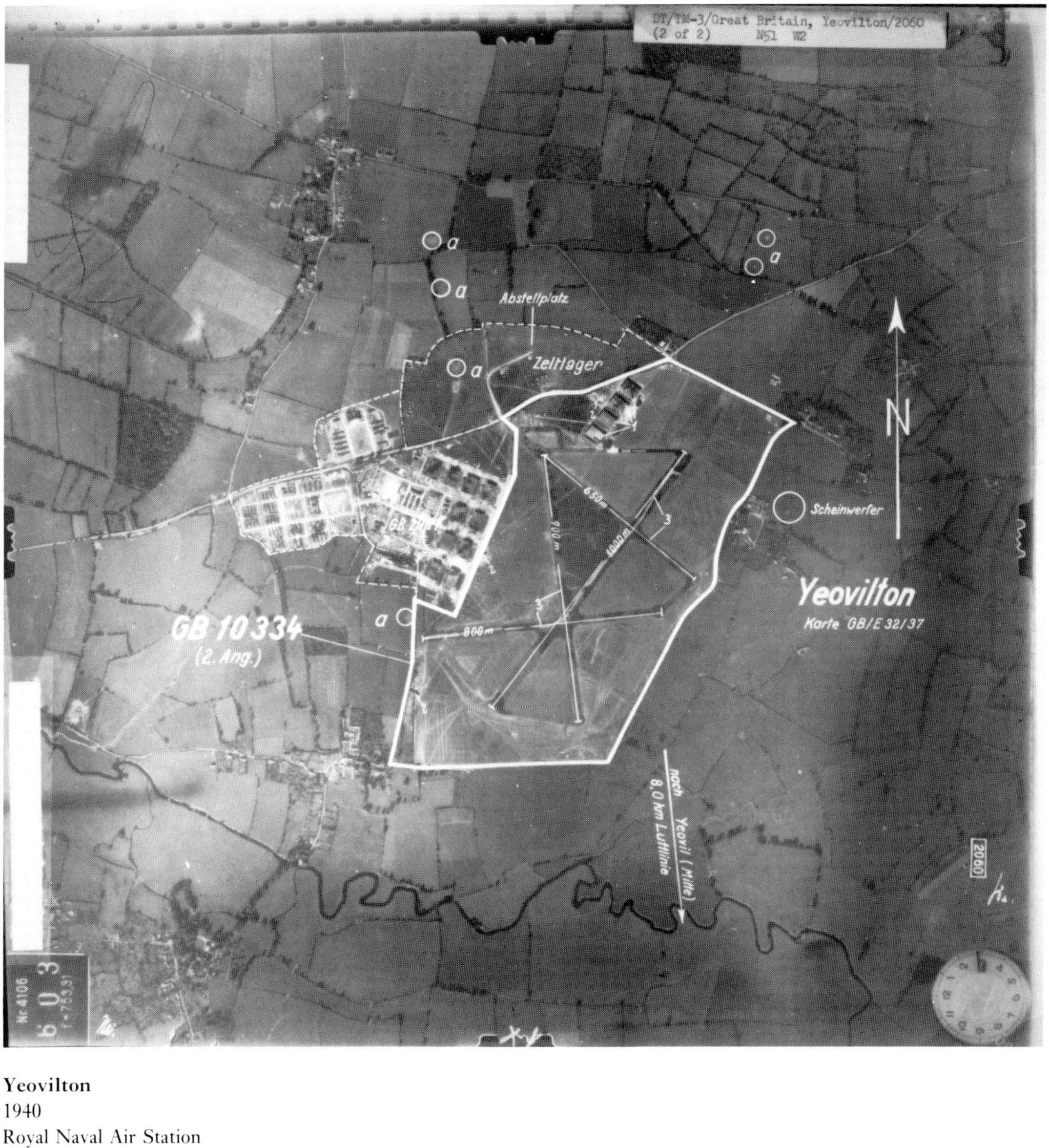

Yeovilton
1940
Royal Naval Air Station
TN 2060
Comment
HMS Heron is now the largest naval air station in the UK. and was commissioned on the 18th of June 1940. The Station was bombed four times during the war, with little damage. The Navy built a decoy airfield four miles to the west of Yeovilton, at Kingsmoor, which successfully fooled the Luftwaffe into dropping four large parachute mines on to the decoy landing runway.

THE ORGANISATION OF THE LUFTWAFFE

The Reichsluftfahrt Ministerium or Air Ministry was in overall command of the Luftwaffe. The Luftwaffe was sub-divided into 4 Luftflotten (air fleets). The largest group was the tactical unit of the Luftwaffe which was known as the Geschwader, which was made up of three or four Gruppen (groups).

A Gruppen had a Headquarters Flight known as a Stab. The commander held the title of Kommodore, his rank being Oberst, Oberst Leutnant or Major.

The Gruppe was sub-divided into three or four Staffel plus a Stab (Head Quarters). Each Staffel was commanded by a Staffel Kapitan holding the title of Kommander, his rank being that of Oberleutnant or Hauptmann.

A Staffel was divided into two each known as a Rotte which would have consisted of three aircraft and two Rotten would have been known as a Schwarm. In each Staffel there were three flights. The Luftwaffe designated Luftflotten 2 and 3 for operations over the United Kingdom. Luftflotten 3 was the section principally concerned with operations over the southern and south-western areas of Britain.

Luftflotten 3 operated from the captured French airfields in north west France, and the headquarters were in Paris. The commander in charge of operations was Fildmarschell Hugo Sperrle. He had gained much of his experience as the German commander of the Condor Legion assisting General Franco to win the Spanish Civil War.

RECONNAISSANCE GROUPS ACTIVE OVER THE UNITED KINGDOM IN JUNE 1940

Aufkiv	2	Reconnaissance Group.BF110,DO17,BF110-MJ,DO17-6M
Aufkiv	13	Reconnaissance Group.BF110,DO17-5F
Aufkiv	122	Reconnaissance Group.BF110,JU88-F6
Aufkiv	123	Reconnaissance Group.BF110,DO17,JU88-4U
KG/40	Group.	Long Range bombers and reconnaissance FW200C-6N
LG/2	Group.	Fighters BF109E; Fighter bomber and reconnaissance, BF110.3x AND L2

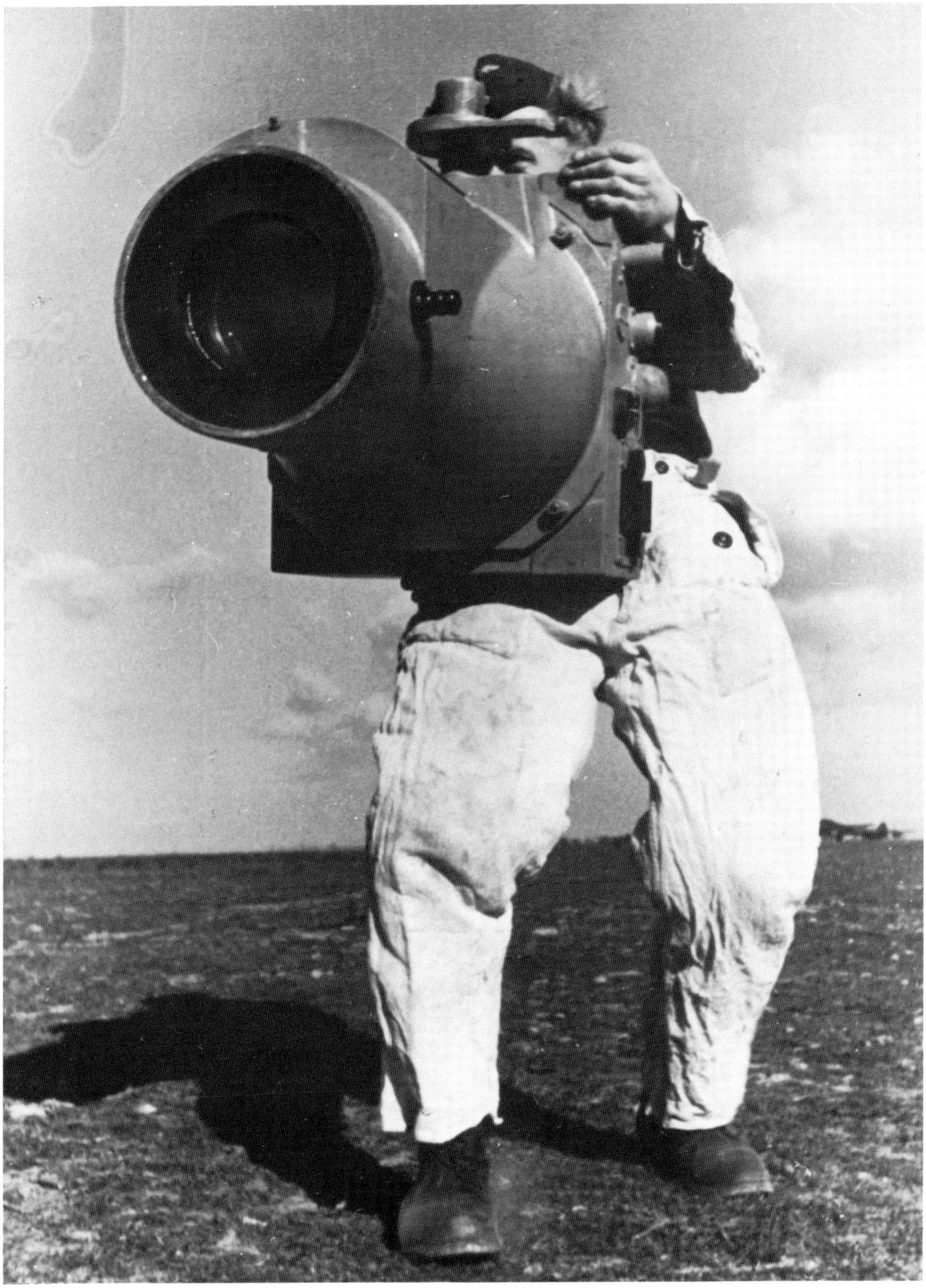

German aerial reconnaissance camera

EQUIVALENT COMMISSIONED RANKS

Luftwaffe	*Royal Air Force*
Leutnant	Pilot Officer
Oberleutnant	Flying Officer
Hauptmann	Flight Lieutenant
Major	Squadron Leader
Oberstleutnant	Wing Commander
Oberst	Group Captain
Generalmajor	Air Commodore
Generalleutnant	Air Vice Marshal
General	Air Marshal
Generaloberst	Air Chief Marshal
Generalfeldmarschall	Marshal of the Royal Air Force

TONS OF BOMBS DROPPED FROM GERMAN NIGHT ATTACKS ON BRITISH CITIES BETWEEN 7TH SEPTEMBER 1940 AND 16TH MAY 1941

City	*Tons of bombs*	*Number of raids*
London	18,800	71
Liverpool	1,957	8
Birmingham	1,852	8
Glasgow	1,329	5
Plymouth	1,228	8
Bristol	919	6
Coventry	818	2
Portsmouth	687	3
Southampton	647	4
Hull	593	3
Manchester	578	3
Belfast	440	2
Sheffield	355	1
Newcastle	152	1
Nottingham	137	1
Cardiff	115	1

Index

PHOTOGRAPHIC REPRODUCTIONS

Black and white reproductions of the photographs in this book are available from the publisher. The picture library includes aerial reconnaissance photographs covering other regions of the United Kingdom and Ireland. For further details and an order form please contact.

Nigel J Clarke Publications
Unit 2, Russell House
Lym Close
Lyme Regis, Dorset. DT7 3DE.
Tel/Fax: 01297 442513